Introspective Rationale: The Odyssey of Theodicy

Mitchell G. Thompson

ISBN: 978-1-5356-1534-1

Contents

Introspective Rationale:
The Odyssey of Theodicy

Chapter 1

Understanding

I.

Existence
noun
1. the fact or state of having **objective** reality

Life
noun
1. the condition that distinguishes animals and plants from inorganic matter, including the capacity for **growth,** reproduction, functional activity, and **continual change preceding death.**

The Human Condition
noun
1. the condition that distinguishes Human Beings from other organic matter, including the **essentials of Human existence (such as intuition, growth, emotionality, individuality, aspiration, and morality)**

Introspection
noun
1. the examination or observation of **One's own mental and emotional processes.**

You are a Human Being before all else.

An essential to introspection is to be open-minded in attempt to dismiss any prior bias. You must acknowledge Yourself for who and what You are: a Human Being. Omit the interethnic conflicts of the world. Disregard gender bias as well. For We are all a part of a single race: the Human race. Embrace the irrefutable nature of what it means to be alive in the here and now – not only as some living being but more prominently a *Human Being*. One stricken with the <u>human condition</u>. A condition that consists of traits of individuality and personal aspirations.

We are all subject to the inherent bias of Our *ego's* deceptive perception. It is the *ego* who behaves under the guise of internal criticism – justifying the relativity of existence in promoting Oneself over the other. Whether it be a lion against a gazelle or some Fortune 500 company against another, Nature establishes the quality of egocentricity as a mechanism for survival at its fittest. Whose survival is predicated on the longevity of the physical self against the sanity of the conscious state. For Life itself exists as a dual manifestation of both a *physical* body and a *spiritual* mind.

Just as the *ego* saves the physical self it plagues the spiritual soul. No different than the very act of living causing the resonance of senescence; the deterioration of Life's cellular makeup due to *time* by aging. An initial step of introspection is the acceptance of *death* as the yin to Life's yang. In that One must first submit themselves to accepting Nature's entropic nature against Life's progressive evolution.

The reality of objective existence is relative to the subjective eyes of the individual. Once the individual *you* ceases to exist so too does the Universe in its infinite potential (relative to *Yourself*). However, the death of the individual doesn't affect the prosperity of the accumulative; for nobody is able to evade the unavoidable state of nonexistence. By accepting *death*, One becomes humbled under a unified notion of certainty in knowing no one is special – not even Our home planet who itself will eventually perish.

Existence precedes Life. To live is to exist. Life, as defined, explores the distinction between organic and inorganic matter. As a collective whole,

Human Beings exist relatively one in the same – anatomically, behaviorally, instinctively, etc. Only as individuals do We vary by the bases of Our <u>human condition.</u>

Time has allowed for Us to acknowledge Our disparateness. The ability to accept the subjective nature of Oneself against the backdrop of Nature's objectivity. Whose subjective qualities of individuality and personal aspiration grant idiosyncratic attributes of distinction. Basic (however so complex) qualities that make you, well, You.

You, the individual, who is infinite in potential; One who exists within the confines of some finite construct. Just as the individual is born so too is their inevitability of death – granted by the linear sovereignty of *time*. For death is merely the opposing face of Life atop the coin of existence. A shining revelation of coping with darkness; instilled by the inherent intuition of the <u>human condition</u>. A condition which is predicated first and foremost on the emotionality aspect of Ourselves.

Emotionality, a key component of the <u>human condition</u>, is not measurable. Even so, a renowned psychologist by the name of Robert Plutchik proposes the concept of **eight basic Human emotions** and **eight derivative emotions** (or **feelings**), to which basic emotions make up more complex feelings.

EIGHT BASIC EMOTIONS

Basic Emotion	Basic Polar Emotion
Joy	*Sadness*
Fear	*Anger*
Trust	*Disgust*
Surprise	*Anticipation*

EIGHT DERIVATIVE EMOTIONS (FEELINGS)

Feeling	Emotional Make-up
1) Optimism	*Joy + Anticipation*
2) Love	*Trust + Joy*
3) Submission	*Trust + Fear*
4) Awe	*Fear + Surprise*
5) Disapproval	*Surprise + Sadness*
6) Remorse	*Sadness + Disgust*
7) Contempt	*Disgust + Anger*
8) Aggression	*Anger + Anticipation*

Our **feelings** are a direct result of specific combinations of basic **emotions.** Modern science allows for the understanding of how certain chemical reactions in the brain are processed to conduct certain emotional states. For example, an individual will feel *joy* as a direct result of a chemical release of dopamine, or *sadness* due to serotonin levels. Another example would be to that of epinephrine or cortisol, which is released due to *anticipation, anger,* or *fear.*

That is not to say Human Beings are the only exception to perceiving emotionality. It seems as though a plethora of non-Human organism share many of the fundamental qualities of complex thinking. Though this seems evident, there exist an obvious gap of applicable intelligence between Ourselves and the rest of the animal kingdom. Generally speaking, most of Life possesses an elementary view of existence with respect to itself. This can be considered a sort of "laser beam" intelligence; where particular problems are met with an equally particular solution. For these solutions are not processed to influence any other problems encountered. In which animals share a simplistic train of linear thought. While Human Beings, on the other hand, possess more of a "floodlight" type of cognition in allowing for complex thoughts to account for complex problem solving. The complexity of this ability poses the act of synthesizing opposing ideas against one another; a natural mechanism for autocorrection. Where Human Beings are capable of using the solution of a particular problem to influence the solution of a completely different problem.

Thus, complex thinking. Thus, the ability for rationale.

Through a multitude of studies on varying animal species, We've uncovered the presence of "cognitive bias" outside of Ourselves. This cognitive bias reveals the existence of certain emotional responses to uncertain outcomes. Also known as *sentience,* this cognitive bias unveils a conscious pattern deviation in judgment at any given time. Simply put, animals tend to live more in the *now,* as a direct result of Darwin's "survival of the fittest" mechanism for natural selection. Perhaps only when an organism is capable of truly expelling the direct threat of its surrounding environment can it intellectually prevail.

That is not to say Our sentient counterparts are incapable of perceiving the many layers of reality. In fact, many non-Human organisms seem to display similar traits of *layered memory* to that of Human Beings:

- **Sensory Memory** – *less than one second*

- **Short-Term/Working Memory** – *less than one minute*

- **Long-Term Memory** - *"forever"*

Long-term memory further encompasses:

1. **Implicit Memory** – *unconsciousness*

2. **Explicit Memory** – *consciousness*

Explicit memory then includes:

1. **Semantic Memory** - *facts/concepts*

2. **Episodic Memory** – *past events/experiences*

Though animals share these many layers of memory input, their "living in the *now*" is directly influenced by *past* experiences – exemplifying **episodic** memory. However, it is in the complexity of **semantic** memory which distinguishes Man from His sentient counterparts.

Sentience is merely the ability to *feel*, perceive, and experience things subjectively, which is shared by Humans and animals alike. The distinction between Human Beings and non-Human Beings stem from the complexity of *sentience*, or cognitive bias, to produce **logic** and **reasoning**. The simplicity in an animal's deviation in judgment is primarily dependent on the threat of the animal's survival. For the sentience of non-Humans is comprised by the *now*, the *present*. While Man maintains the more complex ability to conceptualize beyond the realms of the *present*. In which Our cognition must have an ambient, yet ambiguous, dimension that transcends *time*.

(think on this)

A Human Being nevertheless. Molded by the nurturing of Nature.

Understand there are two types of truths: <u>objective</u> truth and <u>subjective</u> truth. Objective truth is apodictic and irrefutable; *the hue of the sky is blue.* However, subjective truth bears bias. Subjective truth emphasizes personal realities which represent and shape the character (and therefore *ego*) of an individual. Subjective principles from the personal *intuition* of the individual.

Every individual has a concise set of personal beliefs and values based on the development of their own intuition. This personal intuition, in a sense, is the gradual growth of One's psyche over *time* from experience. A result of the nurturing of One's innate nature; molded by environmental influence. How the individual perceives beauty, processes value, justifies morality, and acknowledges Life as a whole.

The characteristics of individuality which We are all composed of. For no one individual is superior than the other, just as no one individual is inferior. The equality of Life stems from the shared *wisdom* of conscientiousness; an appreciation for being alive, here and now, while understanding We are all destined for death.

Whether One identifies under Christianity, Islam, Judaism, Hinduism, Buddhism etc., You must acknowledge the fact that You are a Human Being before all else. Culturally We are surely different, but anatomically We are one in the same. A species who behaves as One.

One who is part of a whole systematic cycle of Life, growth, development, and an inevitable death. Yet the division of Man still exists. What separates Human Beings from the animal kingdom stems from the human condition. A condition that has only recently developed as a result of *time*. A condition that grants the perceptive beauty of Life.

From an objective standpoint, speculation can assume that perhaps We, a species as a whole, have simply not had enough *time* to fully recognize and appreciate Life. For appreciate of anything stems from One's content understanding of its true origins. In which One must ponder; could Life *truly* be appreciated if One is ignorant to its objective origins?

Not to emphasize pessimism, but to introduce introspection; an insight within Ourselves in mass.

Recognize, for what it is, that little voice in the back of Your head which justifies Your daily actions and their consequences. Such is a small voice of internal dialogue which causes reasoning and rationalization when caught at a crossroads.

"Should I go to the gym today?"

"Eh, you could always go tomorrow."

Yes, this voice! The same voice who creates an internal dialogue when One witnesses a homeless man at a traffic intersection wielding a sign, reading,

"Father of 2. Military Vet. Anything helps."

You could stop to offer the man some food or money empathetically, or You could simply drive by and scold the man for his unemployment and inability to provide for his family. The seed of this little voice is One's own personal intuition.

Therefore, the gradual growth of One's psyche over *time* develops their personal intuition; influencing the rationale and reasoning behind their little voice of internal dialogue.

The entirety of personal intuition, however, originates with one word: **faith**. Faith is to prefer spiritual apprehension rather than identifiable proof. That is not to say one is superior to the other, as science cannot "measure" intuition outright. Similarly, the qualities of the <u>human condition</u> are not "quantifiable." Entitling the feeling of **faith** to be a precursor in defining the <u>human condition</u>. One could even argue how **faith** justifies the subconscious and this "little voice" as the "voice of God." The true voice of reasoning.

A miraculous voice of objective intuition. One who gifts Man with the power of knowledge. One who is wise and has evolved in congruence with *time*; a result of eternal progress.

Not to say this is right or wrong, either. Yet, thousands of years ago, in a *time* of inability to fully rationalize the introspection process, wouldn't it just be easier to justify some seemingly "all-knowing voice" as something else? Perhaps a supreme being of omnipotence to dispel any uncomfortable feelings or thoughts? Possibly misconstruing the true differences between <u>objective</u> and <u>subjective</u> truths? Throw in the ingredients of *power* and *imposition* (in the wake of unacknowledged ignorance) and this voice of reasoning becomes the voice of any. A voice predicated on the inflation of the *ego*.

Try to fully conceptualize living in a world where One's thoughts and feelings have no descriptive value – leaving the individual to truly ponder right from wrong. Never knowing if One's moral values are on par with others. In which the basis of One's actions and judgments becomes instinctual rather than communicative. Resulting in the cognitive incapability to objectively articulate One's thoughts and ideas with others. Leaving the intellect of humanity in division.

However, there still exists this basic understanding of right from wrong. An inherent comprehension of moral justification. Without words to articulate understanding, We have always been able to express the innate differences of *good* and *evil;* the primal duality of Life itself. Whether these expressions are instinctual or communicative, We have always found a way to subjectively express the objective nature of known reality. It is only within the unacknowledged ignorance of subjective self-awareness where We become insecure. Ultimately leaving Us in the dark about the totality of objective understanding: for Our vantage point of existence is bound by the subjective parameters of Our <u>human condition.</u> Therefore, We must grasp onto some explanation, anything of rationality, to reach **contentment** in the comprehension of what it means to be alive. A state of **contentment** that sheds light in some form.

Light, illuminating the darkness of Our ignorance.

Even so, the individual is still **ignorant** and will always be wounded with such: the original **sin**. The instinctual nature of **ignorance** subjects Human perception to deception – evidenced by the need for linguistically categorizing "individual truths" as *subjective* instead of all truths reigning in *objectivity*.

For there are far too many unanswered questions that simply cannot be explained.

What is Life?

What is consciousness?

What happens when We die?

Questions such as these lead the Human thought process down a dark path. A path of indifference. A path lingering with ignorance. To be ignorant is not to be stupid or lack intellect. It simply means to lack the knowledge or understanding of a given subject. In modern psychology, the idea of "Argument from Ignorance" proposes the fallacy of informal logic. This idea asserts that a proposition is true because it has not yet been proven false (or vice versa). The result of such a fallacy encourages the progression of cognitive dissonance – halting the progression of formal logic and objective rationale.

For **sin** plagues the mind of all mortal creatures, though more precisely Ourselves, making **ignorance** prevalent in defining the <u>human condition</u>.

II.

The makeup of Our profound <u>human condition</u> gives way to the spiritual acquiescence within every religion.

Understanding religion as the greatest form of coping with Our natural ignorance is essential. Through the existence of an all-knowing deity, ignorance cannot coexist. Yet, inquiring introspection is to acknowledge the innate ignorance of Man. Thusly, to investigate the credibility of any god's all-knowing nature and capabilities.

God
noun
1. (in monotheistic religions) the creator and **ruler** of the Universe and source of all **moral authority**; a supreme being of omniscience (all-knowing), omnipotence (all-powerful), and omnibenevolence (all-loving).

Theodicy
noun
1. the vindication of divine goodness in view of the existence of evil.

"How could *evil* exist under the security of God?"

This is the "Problem of Evil," first posed by the Greek philosopher Epicurus (c. 341 – 270 BCE). The problem stems from both **deductive** reasoning and **evidential** reasoning. The problem with evil is the existence of *contradictions,* which are composed of inconsistent logic. Most religions characterize their "God(s)" as all-knowing, all-powerful, and all-loving. However, by deducing the logic of what One knows they are in turn able to infer with objection.

1. *Evil* exists.

2. God exists and is characterized as all-knowing, all-powerful, and all-loving.

3. There are no bounds to the capabilities of an all-knowing (omniscient), all-powerful (omnipotent), and all-loving (omnibenevolent) God.

4. An omniscient being knows that *evil* exists.

5. An omnipotent being is capable of eliminating or preventing all *evil*.

6. An omnibenevolent being always eliminates or prevents all *evil* for the wholly good.

7. God knows *evil* exists and is capable of eliminating *evil*, so God eliminates all *evil*.

8. *Evil* does not and should not exist.

Thus, the contradiction.

One must either deny the presence of *evil* or ratify this logical deduction. Atheists believe that (2.) should be redefined, as it is illogical to presume God's existence (characterized as such) with the presence of *evil*. For it is impossible to hold the capabilities of omniscience, omnipotence, and *omnibenevolence* without contradiction (in the presence of *evil*). However, theists propose that there are "logical limits" to God's omnipotence. In which an acute ratification of (3.) and (6.) would fix such a contradiction:

1. *Evil* exists.

2. God exists and is characterized as all-knowing, all-powerful, and all-loving.

3. ***There are no *illogical* bounds to the capabilities of an all-knowing (omniscient), all-powerful (omnipotent), and all-loving (omnibenevolent) being.

4. An omniscient being knows that *evil* exists.

5. An omnipotent being is capable of eliminating or preventing all *evil*.

6. ***An omnibenevolent being always eliminates or prevents all *evil* for the wholly good, *unless there is a reason to allow it.*

7. God eliminates and prevents all *evil* that is *logical and possible to eliminate.*

8. *Evil* exists, *but no evil exists that is logically possible to eliminate or prevent, unless there is a good reason to allow it.*

To some, this ratification seems to simply avoid the contradiction rather than provide a solution. For when would there ever be a "good reason" to allow evil? Yet, theists claim God(s) has reasons to allow *evil;* reasons such as the right to **true free will**, granting all possibilities of actions (including *evil* ones). Justifying the presence of *evil* as exemplifying the purest form of free will and thusly Human freedom. True liberation.

Science-based logic questions the physical existence of any supreme being of omnipotence. In that acknowledging the *physical* and *dimensional* presence of any "God" requires **faith,** or spiritual apprehension, rather than a scientific approach. Faith based on the beliefs "written" and "interpreted" by preexisting Human Beings. Individuals stricken with the <u>human condition,</u> as are You, leaving room for personal intuition and bias.

However, the laws of Nature were *not* written by Us.

The laws of Nature are the true laws of "*god.*" The inevitable occurrence of natural events will forever impose the Living. Nature will not kneel to the words of Man, as religion is born on this basis. To all of Life, She is the true omnipotent "being." The natural occurrence of events that creates Life in many forms, including Us. Creating Us for who and what We are; Human Beings. Human Beings with a daunting variable of distinction in Our <u>human condition.</u> The *lack of understanding* for the <u>human condition</u> is the sole source of many of Man's problems. A mere cluster of unanswered and misunderstood qualities that has left Man ignorant to Himself.

But what are these qualities, exactly?

Any innate quality that One would consider to be "Human" in opposition to "non-Human": excelled cognition, intuition, evolved pattern recognition, ability to critically think, aspiration, and One's perception on morality and mortality. These qualities are not independently unique but are qualities that We all share as a grouped species. Especially *pattern recognition;* a profound awareness in Human Beings that, from infancy, cause Our brain to be constantly searching for patterns in the environment. This accolade evolves as it systematically attempts to identify reoccurring events in the effort to make sense of Our surroundings.

As recently stated, the present state of the <u>human condition</u> is relatively new as a result of Our cognitive transcendence over *time.* To truly understand and fully appreciate this concept, One must first truly grasp the origins of Ourselves. For appreciation of anything stems from One's content understanding of its origins.

On October 22, 1996, Pope John Paul II (widely known to most Catholics as "Saint John Paul the Great") states,

> "A basic theme which greatly interests the Church, as Revelation contains, for its part, teachings concerning the **nature and origins of Man**... We know in effect that **truth cannot contradict truth**...Reflection on science at the dawn of the third millennium [observed such] in the domain of inanimate and animate nature, [that] the **evolution of science** and its applications make new questions arise. **The Church can grasp their scope all the better as she knows only their basic aspects.**"
>
> **– JOHN PAUL II OCT. 22, 1996**

John Paul is simply expressing the Church's understanding and interpretation of Nature having evolved in affiliation with the evolution of science. Therefore, as science excels, the more primitive and basic the original scriptures become. He continues;

13

"Consideration of the method used in **diverse orders of knowledge** [including science] allows for the concordance of two points of view which seem *irreconcilable.* **The sciences of observation describe and measure with ever greater precision the <u>multiple manifestations of life and place them on a timeline.</u>** The moment of passing over to the spiritual **is not** the object of an observation of **this type,** which can nevertheless **reveal, on an experimental level,** a series of very **useful signs about the specificity of the human being.** But the experience of metaphysical knowledge, of the **awareness of self and of its reflexive nature, that of the moral conscience...and religious experience, are within the competence of philosophical analysis** ["Theory" of Evolution] while **theology extracts from it the final meaning according to the Creator's designs."**

– JOHN PAUL II OCT. 22, 1996
(https://w2.vatican.va/content/john-paul-ii/it/messages/
pont_messages/1996/documents/hf_jp-ii_mes_19961022_
evoluzione.html)

In essence (as of the year to date, c. 1996), the Pope and the Catholic Church have acknowledged Charles Darwin's Theory of Evolution in *competence* with the religious experience. Meaning both require a degree of **faith**, yet neither reign supreme over the other. One of the world's leading religions has reconciled with the objective truths science has brought forth.

Understand that there is a distinct and significant gap between the birth of spiritual apprehension and the discovery of modern science and mathematics.

Objective truth will forever take precedence over subjective truth. Whether You accept Darwin's proposal or not, You must agree that, over *time,* We have found Ourselves evolving exponentially; from the ability to create and control fire to the discovery of electricity. As evidenced by exponential industrialization, Man has continually evolved in His ability to expand, preserve, and communicate knowledge. Through the advancements of carbon dating, DNA analysis, fossil studies, etc., the scientific community is able to shed some light on the shadows of Man's ignorance.

As an evolving intellect, We have strived to pull Ourselves out of the darkness of ignorance.

Let it be known that modern science is only about five hundred years old. It wasn't until Sir Isaac Newton defines and explains the phenomenon known as *gravity* when Man is finally able to scientifically recount how things *actually* move about and why. The true birth of modern physics, c. 1687 CE, in which Newton releases his publication *Philosophiæ Naturalis Principia Mathematica* ("Mathematical Principles of Natural Philosophy").

Over *time*, Mankind develops significantly. Before the idea of a basic civilization, Our perception of **Life** was no more significant than that of a gazelle in the eyes of a lion. To which I ask You:

Is Life really that bad?

It could be worse.

Life could still be primitive in that the only *Tweeting* going on is from the bird whose eggs You've decided to cook. Accept and realize the simple fact that Life could be much worse. Not necessarily "worse" in conjunction with negativity but more so to that in which Life could be much more challenging for day-to-day survival.

Truly ponder on this idea to appreciate the confines of society, unless You are a true present-day nomad who survives solely on themselves. Otherwise, I ask You to delve further into an introspective odyssey. Understanding the chronological timeline of Our history to appreciate Life and empathize with the rationale of theodicy.

Chapter 2

The Dawn of Man

UNDERSTANDING THE ORIGINS OF Mankind to fully appreciate Our collective existence.

Sixty-five million years ago the dinosaurs face extinction, allowing for the Euarchonta grandorder of mammals to emerge. These proto-primates begin to evolve by the means of a process known as *adaptive radiation* through which many organisms rapidly diversify from a single ancestral species into a multitude of new forms. With the evidentiary achievements in carbon dating, DNA analysis, and fossils study, the scientific community discovers this to be true in the case of Mankind's origin. The use of a taxonomic ranking system allows for a more visual understanding of the chronology and classification of historical biology. From a simple cell paramecium to a complex multicellular organism, the tree of Life reveals its deep rootedness with the intertwining of natural phenomena.

Taxonomic Rank	Name	Common Name
1. Domain	Eukaryota	Cells with nuclei
2. Kingdom	Animalia	Animals
...12. Grand Order	Euarchonta	Tree shrews, lemurs, primates
...18. Family	Hominidae	Human, chimpanzee, gorilla
20. Tribe	Hominini	Genera *Homo* (Human) and *Pan* (chimp and bonobo)
21. Genus	Homo	Human
22. Species	Homo sapiens	Anatomically modern human
23. Subspecies	Homo sapiens sapiens	Behaviorally modern human

If god creates all living creatures on the fifth day and Man on the sixth day, then the lord's chronology of creation parallels that of evolution.

There is no dichotomy between apes and Human Beings. Humans are a type of ape under the taxonomic "subfamily" of *homininae*. Modern studies speculate that between eight and four million years ago there exists a common ancestor between Human Beings and chimpanzees, under the taxonomic "tribe" of *hominini*, known as the CHLCA (Chimp-Human Last Common Ancestor). It is around this point in history that a genetic deviation occurs amongst Our CHLCA mutual-ancestor-species, which results in a microcosmic alteration of chromosomes. Where a certain pair of chromosomes ultimately "fuse" together – effectively creating a genetic mutation to produce the genus *Homo*. All apes of the family *hominidae* possess forty-eight chromosomes divided into twenty-four pairs. Human

Beings, however, have only forty-six chromosomes that divide into twenty-three pairs. A predisposed characteristic following genetic mutation.

For all Humans alike share this pair of "fused" chromosomes that scientists title "Chromosome 2." This *chromosome 2* is the result of an end-to-end fusion of two ancestral chromosomes. Science knows this to be true by the correspondence of *chromosome 2* to two ape chromosomes. Two separate chromosomes found in chimpanzees (who share 98.4 percent of the same DNA as Humans) bear near-identical genome sequences in comparison to the Human *chromosome 2*. Not only this, but also the presence of a second vestigial centromere in *chromosome 2* further exalts such a fusion, along with the remnants of fused telomeres.

This mutation likely happens due to environmental changes, as apes began to shift from the arboreal way of living to a more terrestrial lifestyle due to the thinning of forests (extreme climate change) and availability of ground-based food. The transition from the trees to the ground introduces bipedalism, or "two-feet dependence." This new change in posture allows for the hands of Man-like apes to hang free, enabling the use of *tools*. Birthing innovation.

The first time any creature on earth becomes survival-dependent to traits outside of their species' physical attributes.

The genetic mutation of bipedalism involves changes in the foramen magnum, vertically stretched/lateral flaring hips, and the enlarging of the femur's head (i.e. this mutation results in Human Beings' anatomic evolution). From an environmental standpoint, the thinning of forests is a direct result of the equatorial belt contracting during this time, contributing to the diminishing of fruits and insects – proto-Man's primary diet. These early Man-like apes had to modify their diet on the basis of natural selection. Due to this, and with the help of *tools*, proto-Man began to develop and depend on carnivorous tendencies. This would prove to be more nutritious in helping further evolve the anatomic makeup of Mankind. Tools made up for proto-Man's lack of sharp claws or teeth, as the ape's flat teeth and hands are genetically used for eating fruits and insects (much like modern apes today). Transitioning from an herbivorous diet to a carnivorous without the proper attributes (i.e., sharp teeth) imposes the intuition of Mankind to spark a flame.

Around three million years ago, it is believed that Man began to lose his primitive ape-resembling fur coat. There are many reasons for this genetic change, such as the evolutionary need to regulate body temperature when hunting and *running* – an adaptive new form of terrestrial locomotion (a consequence of bipedalism). Science bases this inquiry on the use of a technique called "the molecular clock," which uses the mutation rate of biomolecules to deduce the time in the past when two or more life forms diverged. It was also around this time that the known fossil AL 288-1, or "Lucy," exists roughly three and quarter million years ago.

The ability to control fire best exemplifies the first time in history where a living being was not dependent on its biological makeup. Fire allows for warmth and cooking, along with security (as fire can also be used to detour predators). Cooking raw meat allows for even more nutrition, which, again, helps further contribute to bioevolution. Not only this, but cooked meat is then easier to chew in making up for Our flat teeth. For *fire*, in form, is merely a microcosmic manifestation of the macrocosmic sun so above.

Time, above all, has allowed for the transcendence of Human cognition. Anatomically modern Human Beings (*Homo sapiens*) evolve more than two-hundred thousand years ago. Over the next hundred thousand years, Man transitions into "behavioral modern Humans," in which We began developing the basic behavior skills of modern Human Beings (*Homo sapiens sapiens*). The Human Beings of today – including Yourself.

It must have also been around this time that We began to wear clothing for warmth, as all Human Beings were nomadic during this period. To survive the harsh winters of the ancient Ice Ages, We depend not on Our biological makeup but on that of artificial enhancement. Science concludes this to be true based off the same technique known as the "molecular clock," for the presence of a new species diverge around this period: clothing lice. Clothing louse differs from head louse to such a degree that they are of a different species entirely. Around one hundred thousand years ago, this new species of louse emerges, only possible with the existence of clothing. From such a conclusion, the evidence of Us utilizing the skins/furs of animals to Our advantage becomes clear. We could now impose Our cunning dominance anywhere on earth by way of manipulating Our homeostasis.

Had it not been for Mankind's inevitable array of advancements, the natural cycle of Life may have maintained order. In a sense that We expel Ourselves from the cycle, breaking from the *animal kingdom*. For We evolve to become a new dominance; the most imposing intellect on earth.

The evidence of the <u>human condition </u>lies within the ruins of ancient Paleolithic **burial** sites of *Neanderthal Man*, a subspecies of the genus *Homo,* which date to the same transition period as the birth of "behaviorally modern Humans."

So what?

To what significance does this provide?

Profound evidence of the paradigm shifting from early hominids to the present genus *Homo.* The act of burying the dead demonstrates the excelled ability in understanding One's own sentience. A way of coming to terms with profound grief. The adults were buried head to head while the children buried near their mother's feet. *Neanderthal Man* was a variance of *Homo sapiens* in that he also obtains the behavioral trait known as the <u>human condition.</u> Our species' cousin, if you will.

Early recognition of One's own sentience transform into primitive signs of expression. Signs of expression prove Man's ability to recognize and cope with the <u>human condition</u>. Burying the dead is a form of expressing grief as creating art is a form of expressing creativity. These early signs of expression allow for Us to empathize with one another and learn from each other. Through the use of basic forms of expression, We become able in productively communicating similar thoughts and ideas. A sharpening of understanding that will lend itself to preserving knowledge. Once knowledge is preserved, it can evolve. A true testament to Our capabilities as a whole. The birth of expression – the transcendence of Human cognition.

The most recent glacial period, known as the "Ice Age," starts around one hundred thousand years ago (during the same time as the emergence of *behaviorally modern Human*s and Our need for clothing). The "Ice Age" is a glacial period that is part of a large pattern of glacial/interglacial periods known as the *Quaternary Glaciation*. Geologists evident such knowledge on the basis of mapping ice-sheets: direction of flow, *meltwater channels* (position of channel in relation to glacier), and sheer size of the ice-sheet(s). According to Milutin Milankovitch, a renowned Serbian scholar, glaciation is caused by cyclical changes in earth's navigation around the sun. These cycles impact the seasonality and solar energy around the earth, thus impacting the contrasts of seasons and their change in climate. These astronomical implications are crucial in understanding the observable nature of the cosmos. The most important knowledge to gain is the productivity of Mankind during this period, although Nature may not have set the best terms. For Man proves His capability in utilizing His profound intellect to defy the affecting elements of Nature. A moment where We, as a species in mass, display traits of overbearing omnipotence.

Finally, ten thousand years ago, the Ice Age comes to an end as the ice-sheets began to recede for the last time. By this time, a far more advanced *Homo sapiens sapiens* emerge to take advantage of the earth's new favorable climate conditions. Through various documented signs of ancient expression, the scientific community has revealed the obvious awareness of Our ancestors' ability to acknowledge and appreciate Our sun, as the sun provides immortal warmth, light, and security. Before the days of fortified communities and shelters, Human Beings reigned inferior when the sun was set. We are not adept to visibly perceive beyond a certain light frequency; where other animals and species can thrive without the security of the sun. Thus, nocturnally crippling the *biological* dominance of Man outright. No matter His intellectual prowess, making the sun and its ever givingness essential for Our survival.

Once the ice-sheets retreat and the conditions of earth are set, the pursuing of agriculture by Man began. So forth that We start to disassociate Ourselves with the nomadic way of hunting and gathering. Agriculture allows for the cultivation of land, which introduces the production of obtaining food in *surplus*. This Neolithic Revolution provides the basis for proto-civilization.

As a result, Human Beings become able in establishing and securing a single area where they can tend to the land. These new concepts began to further drive the need to understand the way of farming One's crops. The preservation of knowledge through collective learning allows for exponential growth in understanding Our sentience. Only made capable by Our extraordinary ability of *pattern recognition* and ability for rationale. Resulting in the allocation of appreciation for Our sun and the heavenly cosmos. For the sun becomes the most adorned object by Man with its ever givingness of light, warmth, security, and nourishment.

Under a unified idea of adornment, Man achieves the ability of spiritual apprehension (**faith**). This unification of *creative thought* (which differs from *instinctual thought,* for animals bear primitive creative skills compared to the human condition) cause for a vast number of proto-civilized populations to maintain a linear train of imaginative thought.

Further questioning and learning about Our surroundings results in the gradual growth of Our Human cognition and a more acute acknowledgement for the human condition. Before the Age of Agriculture, Human Beings were nomadic survival specialists. We had a more intimate connection with Nature (like the animal kingdom) in which We would travel on the basis of such. Where instincts overpower intuition. In these times, Men act as hunting specialists while Women share the equally important role as gatherers/nurturers. This egalitarian lifestyle grants the collective existence of Our species to bear precedence over all things. An egalitarian way of life that would soon be lost at the hands of toxic tribalism.

Once One learns to cultivate crops on a large scale, they become able in settling down within one area – introducing the death of the nomadic way. Graciously so, this began the birth of civilized societies where citizens began to specialize in different trades such as farming, hunting, crafting, etc. (due to surplus). The consequences of specialization place an evolutionary dependence on the skills of others; causing *trade* to become an essential part in furthering Human development. Being able to trade goods allows for the flourishment and sustainability of established societies with varying skilled workers. However, being able to trade starts with the ability to *artistically create.* Creating crafts of materialistic quality, imposing new priorities. Such a society creates a proto-class system; a segregation of "importance" where true egalitarianism cannot thrive. A paradigm shift in equality that will inevitably reprioritize the appreciation for Humanity's collective existence.

However, such a shift does grant a perceptual deviation in Mankind's ***own existence*** from animalistic primitivism to a more distinct species of <u>faith-driven intellect.</u>

Chapter 3

Birth of Religion: A Historical Chronology

I. Mesopotamia - Land of The Civilized Kings

History

AGRICULTURE IS PURELY BASED on the locale of its geography.

By c. 9000 BCE, a century after the last recession of ice-sheets, the land of the Fertile Crescent begins to deliberately grow wild wheat and barley naturally. Only then is agriculture introduced to what will be known as the birthplace of civilization. During this period, archeozoological evidence indicates the domestication of many wild animals including *aurochs;* wild oxen, reigning as one of the largest herbivores of post-glacial Europe (extinct c. 1627 CE). These wild bulls were capable of pulling plows with their fierce voracity, indicating Man's imposition of developmental omnipotence (via domestication). In which Our ability to control and tame such a beast became another feat unmatched by any living being in history. Agriculture with domestication demonstrates the boundless capabilities of Our profound intellect.

All early civilizations settle near river sources as they are the basis of cultivating crops (Tigris/Euphrates, Indus, Hung-Ho, Yellow River, Nile, etc.). These sources are flat and flood frequently enough to provide the nutrient-based silt required for agriculture. Two of the first known civilizations to emerge are *Mesopotamia* and the *Indus River Valley Civilization.*

Archaeologists know much of the former, as both societies developed a formal writing system that provides a source of documentation. However, the language and writing of the *Indus River* people has not yet been deciphered; resulting in the limited knowledge of such people. Only the grandiose beauty of the *Indus River* cities survive (such as Harappa and Mohenjo Daro), which span over the thousands.

Unlike the predictable floods of the Nile, the Tigris and Euphrates flood uncontrollably. These twin rivers reach their lowest levels at the turn of the fall equinox (September – November) and begin flooding at the birth of the spring equinox (March – May). Starting from the eastern mountains of Turkey, the two rivers accumulate the mountainous rain and snowmelt offered by the warm nature of *spring*. This gathered precipitation flows into the two rivers at fluctuating rates annually. So forth that a single yearly flood can carry up to ten times more water than any previous year; contrasting the reliable and predictable annual quantity provided by the contemporary Nile of Egypt. The characteristics of such natural phenomena assume the correlating qualities of ancient civilization's religious pantheon. So forth that the gods of Mesopotamia are represented by the chaotic and unpredictable forces of their regional nature, compared to the less vindictive gods of the Nile in Egypt.

Understanding these flooding cycles is essential in sustaining civilization, especially for the agrarian farmers of Mesopotamia. Without intellectual intervention, societal catastrophe could strike any given year. It is on this basis in which ancient intuitors began to develop a primitive understanding of the cosmos; needing to understand when/where/why/how cyclical changes in Nature occur (affecting agriculture). A primitive understanding of astronomy; articulated by the symbology of astrology over *time* from collective learning.

This intellectual intervention further leads to other inventions such as the implementation of *irrigation,* transforming the sustainability of any agrarian civilization. For *irrigation* (like agriculture) manipulates the natural order of occurring phenomena for the benefit of sustaining society – a cancerous feat of Mankind.

Irrigation allows for the collective manipulation of *water* surplus, which can be directly used to create even more *produce* surplus. An invention of exponential proportions. This surplus of surplus assures a secure food supply and an improved diet – further leading to a period of **influx in dense population** (known as the "Ubaid Period" which lasts from c. 6000 BC – 3800 BC). This period is considered the age of "pre-culture" and "urbanization" where Mankind holds a cultureless existence in servitude to their gods. Compelled only by His ignorance, the instinct of Mankind's profound self-awareness will eventually entice His search for truth.

Expelling ignorance occurs only when One is capable of acknowledging the truth. However, Man, as a whole, has only been able to articulate His words for a short period in His existence. Attempting to acknowledge anything without the words to express that acknowledgement bears difficulty.

Near impossibility.

For it is not until the Sumerian civilization establishes one of the earliest known written languages when Man begins to develop the ability to further articulate His thoughts into *words*. This writing system became known as *cuneiform*, whose original purpose is to document the vast amounts of produce surplus. As civilizations emerge in surplus, so too does their need for keeping track of large quantities of produce (which *cuneiform* offers). From such a system, documentation is born. Such documentation capabilities lead to the creation of **literature** from oral traditions; a new form of expression that would become the basis of understanding the <u>human condition.</u> These oral traditions relay the subjective experiences of past Human Beings. All which stem from the diverse perspectives of a single society (a result of skill specialization). A society where the farmer depends on the knowledge of the intuitor, and the intuitor depends on the produce of the farmer.

Not only did the Sumerians invent a formal, yet isolate, writing system but had also discovered bronze, invented sails to further expand trade (would then teach this technological advancement to the Egyptians), became efficient in basic mathematics/astrology, and are considered the first known people to utilize the wheel effectively.

Much of the knowledge known about this civilization stem from original copies of documents inscribed at the time. Important examples that have been unearthed include:

- *Instructions of Shuruppak* (c. 2600 BCE)

- *Epic of Gilgamesh* (c. 2600 – 2000 BCE)

- *Eridu Genesis* (c. 2300 BCE)

- *A Man and His God* (c. 2100 BCE)

- *Sumerian King's List* (c. 2100 BCE)

- *Code of Hammurabi* (c. 1754 BCE)

- *Enuma Elish (7 Tablets of Creation)* (c. 1500 – 1200 BCE)

The "proto-literate" period of Sumerian writing spans as early as c. 3300 to 3000 BC. Modern science suspects Human Beings as being capable of verbal communication as far back as the first *Homo sapiens*, except the words We "spoke" weren't really "words" but more so mumbled grunts for signal sounds. Therefore, the ancient Sumerian language is considered one of the first "written" languages.

In other words, Man has only been able to verbally articulate His *thoughts* into *words* for about **3 percent** of His existence – dating back to the paradigm shift from early hominids to homo sapiens.

Think about this.

Mankind had been **muted** for **97 percent** of His existence. How could One even begin to address their own ignorance without the words for expression?

Once Man transcends past simple forms of non-written communication (such as primitive art or ritualistic burial), He gains the ability for a more complete way of expression. In turn, We gain the ability to further evolve Our understanding of Our <u>human condition.</u>

In essence, the only feasible means of explaining the unknown is to articulate that of which One *does* know via analogous exemplification. Via

One's subjective perception of Nature in concordance to their surroundings, offered by an innate (however so extreme) ability of pattern recognition. Much like the early cave dwellers one hundred-thousand years ago (and even the Ancient Egyptians to come), Mankind's early intuitors express their thoughts by merely giving meaning to their surroundings. Since the ancient Sumerians' agrarian way of life had to depend on (and in-turn understand) the forces of Nature, their Human-based personification of these surroundings/events became their basis of rationale.

Which is okay! Think about the stages of communication for modern Human Beings. As an infant, the communication barrier is obvious. Infants are unable to express their satisfaction/dissatisfaction through complex sentence structure and definitive meaning. However, they are able to express their ideas through innate behaviors (such as laughing or crying). Over *time*, the infant becomes a toddler and is capable of more basic articulation skills. Given more *time*, the toddler becomes a child whose ability to communicate verbally with simple sentence structure gives more definitive meaning. As further growth and development takes place, so does the Human's ability to further correlate their thoughts to their surroundings.

Take this concept and apply it to the timeline of civilization.

Where ancient Sumer becomes the toddler phase of Human cognition. An era in which basic wedge-shaped iconography claims the furthest advancement in Our communication.

With the profound support of advanced archaeology, ancient Sumerian documents (*Sumerian King's List, Eridu Genesis, Epic of Gilgamesh,* etc.) reveal much of the chronology of ancient Sumer. Beginning with the Ubaid period (c. 6000 – 3800 BCE).

> "After the kingship descended from heaven, the kingship was in Eridu."
>
> – *Sumerian King's List*

Eridu, the far most southern city-state of Mesopotamia, is considered to be one of the oldest cities in the world (inhabited around c. 5400 BCE).

The patron god of Eridu is Enki, the cunning serpent god of water and *wisdom* who holds the divine powers of "Meh" or "Me" meaning "the gifts of culture/individuality" (powers that represent acknowledged self-awareness; Enki does not bestow these powers upon Man quite yet, thus the cultureless Ubaid period). Once the kingship arrives in Eridu, the lands of Mesopotamia become used to cultivate produce *for* the gods. For Mankind is thought to have been enslaved by the gods, worthy only of laborious inquisition. Mesopotamia; the eden of Our enslavement.

The Sumerian story of *Inanna and the Huluppu Tree* explains how the goddess of fertility, love, and war, Inanna, takes the essence of Mankind (via the "Huluppu Tree" or the "Tree of Life" which traditionally originates in Eridu) to her home in Uruk (biblically known as Erech; possibly named after *auroch* to resemble the city's power/strength). Being a patron goddess of Uruk, Inanna steals the divine powers of "Me" from Enki and bestows them on her people – historically corresponding to the ending of the "Ubaid" period of servitude. This is one of many accounts where Mankind receives His *cultural* powers of "Me" in that later accounts recall the bestowing of such powers by divine demi-gods. By receiving the power of "Me," the people of Uruk became "like the gods" in their new intuitive ways of acknowledged **self-awareness**. This gave birth to culture in a period known as the "Uruk" period (c. 3800 – 2900 BCE).

By c. 3500 BCE, Mesopotamia has established societies where the creation of city-states came to be (Eridu, Ur, Uruk, Kish, Lagash, etc.). Each city-state holds a temple at its center, known as a ziggurat, which emphasizes both the importance of religion and awe-striking political power. These city-states are self-governed, but all of those in the region of Mesopotamia carry a similar form of culture and thus polytheistic worship (comparative to the many forms of Christianity; Catholic, Protestant, Baptist, etc.). Each ancient city honors its own patron god, halting the unification of a state ruled Mesopotamia, leaving the region divided and exposed. However, people of this region collectively appease to the belief in their ancient gods as creating the earth and utilizing Man solely as their servants.

As stated, each city-state belongs to a particular god or goddess; such as Anu, god of the Heavens, belonging to Uruk (along with Inanna); Enki, god of water and *wisdom*, reigning supreme in Eridu; or Nanna (Sin), god of the moon, residing in the city of Ur (home of Terah, father of Abram). The Uruk period is considered the birth of culture due to the extraordinary advancements in civilization. The completion of a written language (literacy), the implementation of a structured class system, the establishment of trading routes, proficiency in mathematics (based off the number "sixty" known as a sexagesimal math system; hence the measurement of longitude and latitude, degrees of three-hundred sixty, sixty minutes of an hour, sixty seconds in one minute, etc.), effectively imposing regulations on society (comprised primarily of agrarian farmers); the list goes on and on. Most importantly, the Sumerians retain a proto-understanding of astronomy on the basis of astrological observation. All due to an abundance in produce, allocating for "leisure spending" of *time*; a quality further expanded by later Persian-Greek philosophy.

As a result of a complete written language, the Uruk period brought forth the first written records of religious tradition – as early as c. 3500 BCE. These advancements in cultural and social stability led to an urban revolution, where Uruk is allowed to flourish at a time with as many as forty-thousand inhabitants.

Most of these inhabitants, as addressed, are farmers. Farmers who are now a part of a formed class structure:

- *Lugal* [kings]
- *ensi* [high priest(s)]
- merchants/nobles
- artisans
- scribes
- farmers
- slaves

During the Ubaid period, the *ensi* or "high priest" is considered the intermediary between Man and His god, interpreting the will of the gods by their occurring presence in natural phenomena. In doing so, the *ensi* are responsible for the construction of irrigation canals and accounting for the annual flooding (considered to be religious duties). For the gods gave Man the tools for agriculture and would flood His plains with nourishment. Resulting in the high priest holding apogeic power of kingship.

Yet, during the Uruk period (when Man receives the power of "Me" or "culture"), the *ensi* seize kingship to the *lugal* or "big Man" who originally only seize temporary power in a time of war/anarchy (early form of martial law). Sumerian history up to this shift, much like the interpreted divine spark of "Me," is directly analogous to that of the biblical Genesis, chapters 1 through 6; from *creation*, to *the fall of Man*, to *the flood*. Much like the gifts of "Me" plaguing the perception of Mankind, the forbidden fruit from which Eve had ate made Adam and Eve "like God" (Genesis 3:5) to initiate *the fall of Man*. Once We "...knew of [Our] nakedness" (Genesis 3:7), the corruption of evil became evident, resulting in the biblical deluge to cleanse the world of its profound wickedness.

Coincidentally enough, there were many fluctuations in rising water levels of the Tigris and Euphrates during this time in history (due to the chaotic nature of the two rivers) that leads to a series of floods. Most notably the flood of the biblical deluge that ended the Uruk period in c. 2900 BCE.

> "Then the flood swept over...
> After the flood had swept over, and the kingship had descended from heaven, the kingship was in Kish."
> — *Sumerian King's List*

This era-ending flood introduces the Early Dynastic period of Sumer (c. 2900 – 2350 BCE). Kish, one of Sumer's most northern city-states, holds evidence of the earliest confirmed ruler on the *Sumerian King's List*, Enmebaragesi, whose son, Aga of Kish, rules in contemporary with the renowned king of Uruk, named Gilgamesh. The shift in power from *ensi* to *lugal* introduces patriarchy in which a king appoints an heir (his son) to his throne. Patriarchy; the death of egalitarianism.

However, Gilgamesh isn't the first post-deluvian king of Uruk. His father, Lugalbanda, is predecessor of the post-flood "first founder of Uruk," Enmerkar. The three separate stories of *Enmerkar and the Lord of Aratta, Enmerkar and Ensuhkeshdanna [Lord of Aratta],* and *Lugalbanda and Enmerkar* (c. 2100 BCE) are known to be the first written epics of history (predating Homer's *The Iliad* and the *Odyssey* nearly fifteen hundred years). These stories tell the tale of Uruk's divine dominance over its neighboring cities (exemplified through the city of Aratta). Much like the *Odyssey,* the last entry of this ancient epic depicts the events of Lugalbanda's *journey* in delivering a message to the divine goddess Inanna, who is in Aratta at the time (as the people of Aratta have now submitted to Enmerkar). The message is for Inanna to come back to Uruk to assist Enmerkar, who is under attack by "Semitic speaking people." Archaeologist believe these early post-flood events took place between c. 2900 – 2500 BCE (including the reign of Gilgamesh, c. 2700 BCE).

By c. 2500 BCE, Mesopotamia is split between the Akkadians of the north and the Sumerians of the south. The events that take place in the last story of *Lugalbanda and Enmerkar* perhaps speak of the disputes between the two regions – as the Akkadians are a "Semitic speaking people." Although the Akkadians develop a written language, its form is adopted and adapted from the Sumerian cuneiform script. During this dynastic era, neighboring wars are fought amongst the city-states of Mesopotamia on the basis of conflicting resources (land, water, trade-routes, etc.), resulting in a constant shift of power/control over the region.

One city of kingship that has been omitted from the *Sumerian King's List* are the dynasties of Lagash – whose patron god is Ninurta; "champion of the gods." The first king of Lagash, Ur-Nanshe (c. 2500 BCE), conquers all of Sumer and annexes Kish (who would regain their independence under the only woman on the *Sumerian King's List,* Kubaba). Ur-Nanshe's grandson, Eannatum, then leads an army to force subjugation on their neighboring rival city-state of Umma. The triumph over Umma is elaborately depicted via Eannatum's fragmented *Stele of Vultures,* containing a "historical" face and a "mythological" face. The historical face depicts the conquest of Umma, while the mythological face tells the fragmented fable of Ninurta's influence in assisting Eannatum.

Conquest, appeasement. Conquest, appeasement. Until the unification under Sargon the Akkadian, more famously known as **Sargon the Great** (c. 2334 BC – 2279 BCE).

According to his known autobiography the *Legend of Sargon,* Sargon is illegitimately born to a priestess of Inanna (who are not *allowed* to bear children). Unable to reveal her pregnancy, she could not keep her son. Thus, setting the bastard child adrift the Euphrates river in a basket; where he would be found by Akki, the gardener for Ur-Zababa – king of Kish. It is told that Sargon is raised by the blessing of Inanna to align himself with the common people of Mesopotamia rather than the *lugal* and elite. This story is a direct parallel to that of the biblical Moses; born illegitimately from a mother who set him adrift the Nile, only to be found by royalty. As both are raised in the very society that they would one day challenge alongside the view of the oppressed.

> "[Sargon,] whose father was a gardener of Ur-Zababa, became king, the king of Akkad, who built Akkad."

Sargon the Great is given credit for establishing the first known empire in history – though previous *lugals* had unified Sumeria under one rule. The influence of the Akkadians on Sumerian culture brings forth a ratification in their religious worship. For example, the Akkadian city of Babylon is established in introducing a new god to the pantheon named Marduk. Also, the moon god of Ur became known as the Akkadian "Sin" from the previously Sumerian "Nanna." Just as Inanna, goddess of Uruk, became known as Ishtar, and Utu the sun god is renamed as "Shamash." This is evidence of a reoccurring theme throughout Man's history when conquest, consolidation, and expansion occur. In which the ideas of yester are recycled in false originality.

Sargon would go on to relieve the throne to his sons after establishing his empire's capital of Akkad. Sargon also claims a daughter by the name of Enheduanna: the first historically known author by name. Before Enheduanna, the precision of "who wrote what" seemed to elude archaeologists from the vast vagueness of early documentation. Enheduanna is crowned the highest priestess (and wife of the *ensi)* of Ur (supposed home of Terah and Abram), granting her spiritual authority over a unified Mesopotamia. So forth that she composes hymns for each Sumerian city's ziggurat and their patron god, which ultimately deifies the city's ziggurat temple as the gods themselves. All in all, Enheduanna's *Sumerian Temple Hymns* extrapolate a trove of corresponding descriptions/depictions of the Sumerian pantheon (which is adopted by Sargon and the Akkadians), only to be preserved/added onto, not dismantled/overrun.

By the time Sargon's grandson Naram-Sin comes to power (c. 2190 BCE), the stream flow of the Tigris and Euphrates began to lighten up. Studies of sediments within the Persian Gulf reveals the effects of a drought occurring between c. 2100 – 2000 BCE. Any damage inflicted to the agricultural system (whether it be raids, bureaucratic mismanagement, or inattentive management) would result in drastic produce shortages.

> "Uruk was defeated and the kingship was taken [by] the armies of the Gutians."
>
> *– Sumerian King's List*

Introducing the last people an individual would want to be in charge during a economically sensitive time: a nomadic tribe called the Gutians. These cultureless "barbarians" would routinely commit hit-and-run raids on the city-states of Mesopotamia. Traveling became unsafe (affecting trade) along with mending crop fields, crippling the economy of Sumer/Akkad. Before too long, these nomadic people had become successful in crippling the Sumerian/Akkadian economy enough to ensure anarchy. By c. 2150 BCE, the

Guti conquer Uruk and sweep through Sumer, eventually destroying the city of Akkad completely (around c. 2115 BCE; whose remains are yet to be found).

With that being said, not all city-states are supplanted by the Guti. As they swept through Mesopotamia and onward to Akkad (center of Akkadian Empire; north of Sumer), the Gutians inevitably establish Akkad as their own "dynastic center place." This would only further distance themselves from maintaining the conquered lands of southern Sumer. As a result, previously conquered Sumerian cities (such as Uruk and Ur) began to retain a state of self-governing autonomy by simply paying tribute to the Guti. The second dynasty of Lagash (omitted from *Sumerian King's List*), would be another one of those cities to pay tribute and thusly thrive during the Gutian reign.

Before Akkad had completely fallen to the Gutians, a contemporary of the last king of Akkad is Ur-Baba (c. 2164 – 2144 BCE): the first king of the second Lagash dynasty. Ur-Baba would go on to bear a daughter, Ninalla, who would marry the prosperous ruler known as Gudea (perhaps named in appeasement to Gutians). Gudea (c. 2144 – 2124 BCE) is one of the most esteemed rulers in Sumerian history, giving the people of his reign twenty prosperous years of peace. Gudea is considered "a model of piety and virtue, working tirelessly for the gods and the welfare of his people." His reign includes building social structures (temples, walls, etc.), allowing for art to flourish (including many famous alabaster busts of Gudea himself), and revolutionizing social reform (hindering to the common person). In the myth *The Building of Ninurta's Temple* (which is depicted on what are known as the Gudea Cylinders) Gudea is described as, "...providing protection for the orphan against the [rich] and provided protection for the widow against the powerful. He had the daughter become the heir in the families without a son." Above all else, Gudea isn't a *lugal* "king" nor did he intend to represent himself as one. In part because he wasn't of true royal blood, as he simply married into royalty, warranting no need for an heir apparent order of succession (although Gudea's son does succeed his father's throne). On the *Seal of Gudea*, Gudea is portrayed as bareheaded and without his crown (the famous "shepherd's hat"); hands raised in reverence. By the standards of Sumerian culture, these qualities resemble that of any "mortal Man," meaning Gudea intentionally chose to not be falsely represented in deified form (as past *lugals* had done; Enmerkar, Etana of Kish, Gilgamesh, etc.).

Gudea's son, Ur-Ninurta (c. 2120-2113 BCE) reigns in contemporary with Utu-Hegal of Uruk (the only king of Uruk's fifth and final dynasty). Utu-Hegal is the *"lugal* chieftain" of the city of Uruk during the end of the Gutian reign. In fact, Utu-Hegal (in succession with his son-in-law Ur-Nammu) is credited with the expulsion of the Guti from Mesopotamia in the myth *The Victory of Utu-Hegal.*

> "Then the army of Guti was defeated and the kingship was taken to Uruk."
>
> *– Sumerian King's List*

Once the kingship arrives in Uruk, Utu-Hegal appoints his son-in-law Ur-Nammu as governor of Ur (patron home of the biblical Terah and Abram). This sparks what is known as the "Sumerian Renaissance" which occurs during the third dynasty of Ur. During this renaissance, Ur-Nammu reigns (c. 2112 – 2098 BCE) and has the Ziggurat of Ur begin its construction [one of the only preserved Sumerian ziggurats in existence today]. Ur-Nammu is also credited with conquering the last king of the second dynasty of Lagash en route to conquer all of Mesopotamia in hopes of reviving a "Sargonic" dominance. Most importantly, Ur-Nammu creates the first complete written code of laws: "The Code of Ur-Nammu." Although an older code of law is constantly referenced in ancient Sumerian texts called "The Code of Urukagina" (Urukagina was the last king of the first dynasty of Lagash), no physical form of this law code has been unearthed, granting Ur-Nammu's law code as the oldest written set discovered (pre-dating the famous "Codes of Hammurabi" by almost a half of a millennium).

By c. 2095 BCE, Ur-Nammu is killed in battle and succeeded by his son, Shulgi. King Shulgi (c. 2094 – 2047 BCE) is often accredited with implementing his father's code of laws and completing the construction of the great ziggurat of Ur. Perhaps his most known accomplishment includes a revision in scribal affairs, including the numerous praise poems directed towards the king – most notably "Shulgi-D" the self-praising psalm of Shulgi.

Shortly after his reign, Shulgi's great-grandson Ibbi-Sin becomes the last ruler of the Sumerian Renaissance. Once having ruled all of Mesopotamia, the Ur III dynasty is left with only their tribal city-state by the end of Ibbi-Sin's reign. Around the year c. 2004 BCE, Ur is sacked and conquered by a neighboring civilization known as the Elamites (with help from the north-western Amorites). This period of distraught is accounted for by what is known as the *Lament for Ur*. To consequently follow Ur's demise was the plunging of all of Mesopotamia into a "dark age." Perhaps it is during to this Mesopotamian "dark age" where the biblical Abram sought refuge outside of his home city in Ur.

Centuries of warring amongst the city-states of Mesopotamia came to end by the illustrious Amorite king Hammurabi (c. 1792 – 1750 BCE) of Babylon, which had been a prosperous Akkadian city post-Sargon's reign. Hammurabi's predecessors had done little to expand the regional dominance of Babylon. Be that as it may, at the height of Hammurabi's power, he is able to force the king of Assyria (a prominent power at the time) to pay tribute to his kingdom of Babylon. Within a few years, Hammurabi becomes successful in uniting all of Mesopotamia under his rule. Once established, he implements his famous "Hammurabi Code of Laws," which are considered to be heavily influenced by the previously known "Code of Ur-Nammu." For the standards of the time, Hammurabi's laws are considered to be reasonably just and humane ("...an eye for an eye..."). Sadly, his unified kingdom of Babylon unravels at the hands of his successors. These succeeding kingships are tainted with catastrophic uprisings that led to the vast abandonment of the controlled city-states of Sumer. Soon after, the Babylonians are conquered by the nomadic Hittite Empire who resemble much of the same characteristics as the Sargonic Akkadians (in terms of adopting/adapting the indigenous script, literature, art, and religion of the Babylonians rather than eradicating them all together). Biblical testimony refers to the origins of the Hittites as "dwelling in the [north of Canaan]," which proves historically/geographically accurate. By c. 1531 BCE the Hittite king Mursili I conquers

Babylon. These Hittite nomads will only reign supreme until their ultimate demise brought on by neighboring tribes and sea-raiders in c. 1200 BCE – including the biblical Philistines and the opposing Assyrians.

With the collapse of the Hittite Empire, the prominent power of Assyria began to rise under the leadership of Assyrian king Tiglathpilesar I (c. 1100 BCE) after his own conquest at Babylon. This early Assyrian conquest sets the tone for their success to come. By the ninth-century BCE, king Assurnasirpal II reigns over the Assyrians as an aggressive military genius. The conquest of the Assyrians is so hated by chroniclers of the Old Testament, claiming these foes "as brutal and violent as they were numerous." An eighth-century ruler of this empire took the name of Sargon II, exposing a long-held Sargonic influence over the region of the Middle East in its totality. Sargon II establishes an Assyrian capital in the ancient city of Khorsabad, only for his son Sennacherib (c. 705 – 681 BCE) to later move the capital to the glamorous ancient city of Nineveh (known for its fine Assyrian artwork including "The Winged-Bulls of Nineveh"). Many documents were found at Nineveh in which depict the destruction of Babylon by Sennacherib, who himself quotes,

> "The city and its houses, from its foundation to the top,
> I destroyed, I devastated, I burnt with fire... Through the
> midst of the city I dug canals. I flooded its site with water,
> and the very foundations thereof I destroyed."

The destruction of Babylon reinforces the notion of conquest under appeasement. By enforcing such dominance, the Assyrians are able to besiege the kingdom of Judah by c. 701 BCE. Under the sovereignty of Hezekiah, King Sennacherib extorts tribute from Jerusalem to ensure the Assyrians would not utterly destroy the holy city. This event is further emphasized and explained not only by the Assyrians in their famous *Sennacherib's Prism,* but also by the Israelites in the second biblical book of Kings (2 Kings 18:13), depicting the invasion of Judah by the Assyrians. This form of imperial order reframes its primitive form from the lackluster attempt by the Gutians to sustain imposition through a central authority.

All while the Assyrians take charge, the remnants of the Babylonian Empire became absorbed into the Semitic Chaldeans; including the regions of southern Sumer and the Levant. Remember, this constant conquest, appeasement, conquest, appeasement is cycling about throughout a core region – the (soon to be *not* so) Fertile Crescent.

The Neo-Babylonian group of Chaldeans remain subject to the Assyrians yet begin to slowly recover (much like the Sumerians of Ur and Uruk during the Gutian oppression). By the end of the seventh century BCE, the Neo-Babylonian Empire re-establishes themselves under the leadership of Nebuchadnezzar "Destroyer of Nations" at the fall of Nineveh in c. 612 BCE. The re-institution of Babylonian rule reinstates the sovereignty under Marduk and dismisses the notion for any religious tolerance. For the Babylonians besiege Jerusalem; where Psalms 137:1 laments, "By the rivers of Babylon, there we sat down, yea, we wept, when we remembered Zion." A toll of loss, as the children of Judah were imprisoned by the tens of thousands under the word of Nebuchadnezzar.

Then, by c. 539 BCE, the great Cyrus of Persia succeeds in conquests for Babylonian appeasement. Where instead of destroying the city of Babylon, like the Sargonic Akkadians and Hittites before them, the Persians preserve the city as a part of their empire. Only to be eventually conquered by the great Alexander of Macedonia. Thusly, bringing an end to the land existing of the supposed "civilized kings."

<u>Religion</u>

The Sumerian pantheon reveals itself throughout the continuum of the Middle East.

It is the people of ancient Sumerian Mesopotamia who believe in a core ideology of Creation; one which tells the story of Man's origins in relation to their gods' existence. The Sumerians regard the Universe as *"anu-ki"* or "heaven-earth" in which the cosmos make up a primordial-like sea. These primordial waters are ruled by Tiamat (Nammu), who uses the "fresh waters of Apsu" to give birth to the *four creator gods.* Two of the four *creator gods,* **An**shar and **Ki**shar, go on to create the *seven gods who decree fate:*

1. Anu – God of heaven (city of Uruk)

2. Nihursag (Ki) - Goddess/Mother of Earth (city of Kish)

3. Enlil – God of wind; separator of the *anu-ki* "heavens and the earth" (city of Nippur)

4. Enki – God of "Me"; serpent of *wisdom* and freshwater; "creator of Man" (city of Eridu)

5. Nanna (Sin) – Moon god (city of Ur)

6. Inanna – Goddess of love and war; fertility (city of Uruk)

7. Utu – Sun god of justice; patron of Mankind (city of Larsa)

A common motif throughout Sumerian religion is the surpassing of a patron deity's power and influence in relation to its neighboring city-states. For example, during the Ubaid period (pre-culture), it is likely that no worship of specificity was in place – for the agrarian farmers need only to adorn the sun and its ever givingness (so perhaps an early form of Utu).

However, once culture began to thrive and Mankind's ability to further articulate His thoughts began, the emergence of specificity arose (evident by the Uruk period and thus specificity in adorning Anu, patron god of Uruk). Introducing specification allows for a narrowing of rationalization.

> "What is helping our agriculture besides the sun? Obviously, the annual flooding...perhaps the *bull* has turned out to be a fine mender of the fields...but hmm? What else?"

This linear thought process would begin a path of unintentional introspection: portraying One's own innate characteristics through the creative mechanism of deifying and anthropomorphizing. An attempt to subjectively articulate objectivity. By assigning characteristics or "roles" for the unexplained phenomena of Nature (One's surroundings), early intuitors unknowingly began to unravel a rationale for objective introspection, further illuminating *wisdom* upon the ignorance of Our human condition.

This introspective shift compels Mankind to transition His once primitive ideals of "cosmic God(s)" through the subjective comprehension of Nature and Her many manifestations.

A paradigm shift of arrogance. Where Man creates god(s) in His own image.

This transcendent perception propels Mankind's collective understanding of Our human condition. So forth that We began to deify Nature with Our own Human characteristics. An instinctual response to the innate ignorance that naturally plagues Our soul; relating an idea to One's own personal experiences to further sympathize and allow empathy to permeate their final judgment.

> "It's sort of like that one time when I –"

Think back on the episodic distinction between animals' "laser beam" intelligence and Our "floodlight" intelligence. Mankind's ability for complex thought is a direct correlation to complex solutions. This complex problem solving, seemingly secular to Human Beings, displays the ability of using the solution of a particular problem to influence the solution of a completely different problem (capable by Our awesome *pattern recognition*). Relating past solutions to new problems, over *time*, grants intuitive growth. The difference in the complexity of episodic memory bridges the intellect gap between Human Beings and the *animal kingdom*.

What better way to further understand the nature of unreconcilable phenomena than to compare them with the patterns of One's own instinctual tendencies? In an attempt to understand how or why the sun rises every morning and sets every night. Trying to comprehend the shortening of days that occurs at the turn of autumn's eve (delivering the fall). The falling of leaves and balding of trees. Where Mother Earth begins to turn cold and retreat with death. Only for the rain of frozen waters to cover the plains with a frigid white blanket. The wintry white snow of stoic content, capable of soul submission from Man or animal, plant or seed. As death is known to be inevitable yet is forced upon by *winter's* clasp.

That is until the days progressively prolong, allowing the snow sheets to subside – bearing water as the plains remain in a fetal state. While the fertile plains await their awakening, they are slowly reborn. The trees grow leaves as the seeds of Nature blossom; portraying the rebirth of Life. Only for the turn of the spring equinox to ensure the cycle has begun again as light triumphs darkness. A continual cycle of seasonality; understood originally by their organic characteristics in representing both Life and death.

The simplicity in ancient rationale stems from a basic comprehension of Nature's objective nature. Once the age of specificity came to be, so does the influx in anthropomorphic deities and their origins. During the Uruk period (c. 3800 – 2900 BCE), it is speculated that Anu claims head of the pantheon, being the patron god of Uruk and "father of the gods." However, once the dynastic periods arose, the son of Anu, Enlil, takes his father's throne as the new head of the pantheon. Enlil's patron home was that of Nippur; the *central* most city in all of Sumer. For the majority of Sumerian literature acknowledges Enlil's divine kingship, until the rise of Babylon (c. 1800 BCE). Once Babylon came to prominence, so does their patron god Marduk; the all-powerful sky **god of war**. Evidence of this shift is resembled by Marduk replacing Enki's role as "creator of Mankind" in the Babylonian Bible-equivalent *Enuma Elish (7 Tablets of Creation)*. Once the Hittite Empire collapses around c. 1200 BCE, the Assyrians rise with imperial power. By c. 1100 BCE, the Assyrian king Tiglathpilesar I conquers Babylon and grants sovereignty to Assyrian rule and thus their favored god of worship, Ashur, who is literally the Assyrian version of Enlil (and the name of one son of the biblical Jacob) only renamed by the Assyrian language. In which Enlil retains his reign at the head of the pantheon, once again, until the conquest of the Neo-Babylonians of the Chaldeans takes place, resulting in the divine transition back to Marduk.

Back and forth; back and forth.

These series of shifts in divine kingship are obvious in their chronology of documentation: depending on who is in power at the time, their testimony is considered truth.

Nonetheless, the core ideology of Sumerian religion remains relatively constant. They envision the Universe as a closed dome surrounded by primordial saltwater. The god Anu's form is represented by the "dome-shaped heavens," while Ninsurhag (Ki) is acknowledged as the physical earth. Enlil, son of *anu-ki* and god of wind, is observed as the *air* or *wind* in representing the force of separation between his parent deities. When this separation occurs, Enlil symbolically takes the throne from his father, Anu, by taking away the earth (Ki) from the heaves (Anu). Once head of the pantheon, Enlil entrusts the "powers of Me" or the "powers of the gods" to his brother Enki, cunning serpent god of water and *wisdom* (for now, Enki simply holds onto the power).

> "The [lower class] gods had to dig out the canals
> Had to clear channels, the lifelines of the lands,
> The [lower class] gods dug out the Tigris river bed
> And then they dug out the Euphrates."
>
> (*Atra-Hasis*)

Evidence in Sumerian religion offers the outward portrayal of their society's qualities in the form of a patriarchy/class system amongst the gods. After thousands of years of strenuous work, the "lower-class" gods (who symbolically account for the labor/maintenance of the existing world) began to complain to Enlil and hold a strike outside of his dwelling. Enlil, with the help of Anu and Ki, devise a plan to relieve the gods of this arduous task by passing on the burden through domestication [symbolic for Our imposition of domestication upon the "lower intellect" of beings; as in utilizing *aurochs (bulls)* to help relieve Us from the burdensome aspects of the agrarian lifestyle]. Through the help of the birth goddess Ninmah and her clay, Enki is able to assist in the Creation of Man.

After the conception of Man, the gods utilize Him through domestication in slavery; with His efforts providing both Himself and the gods sustainability. It is during this time that the kingship descends from heaven to Eridu. During this antediluvian period reigns the *Apkallu*, known as the "seven demi-god fishermen of Enki; the seven sages of the pre-flood." Only then did the sprouting of the Huluppu occur, forcing Inanna to take the "Tree of Life" to Uruk. Once the tree is established in Uruk, Inanna is able to steal the divine powers of "Me" from Enki and bestow them upon her people of Uruk.

Now that Mankind has the powers of "Me" and culture, He inevitably irritates His gods (most notably Enlil). During these efforts, the influx of surplus increases the population of Man, which began to grow so much that "[Our] noise began to trouble Enlil's slumber."

> "The country was as noisy as a bellowing bull
> The god [Enlil] grew restless at [Our] racket,
> Enlil had to listen to [Our] noise, He addresses the [other] gods,
> 'The noise of Mankind has become too much,
> I am losing sleep over their racket;
> Give the order that [plague] shall break out."
>
> *(Atra-Hasis)*

Plague breaks out but is eventually upheld as the gods' servants prevail in pleading with Namtar (the god of sickness). Only for the population of Man to increase once more, again bringing about "too much noise." These fluctuating mood swings of Enlil's disturbance at Our "noisiness" continues as he afflicts Man with droughts,

"When the second year arrived
They had depleted the storehouse.
When the third year arrived
The people's looks were changed by starvation.
When the fourth year arrived
Their upstanding bearing bowed,
Their well-set shoulders slouched,
The people went out in public hunched over.
When the fifth year arrived
A daughter would eye her mother coming in;
A mother would not even open her door to her daughter...
When the sixth year arrived
They served up a daughter for a meal,
Served up a son for food."

(*Atra-Hasis*)

This drought is foiled by Enki when he feeds his starving people with large quantities of fish, eventually restoring Man's fate. Enlil began to be so enraged by Enki's interference that he instructs the deluge of Mother Earth (Ki). Preparing for the final demise of Human existence, Enlil instructs Enki (god of fresh water) to eradicate that of his own creation. Enki responds with, "Why should I use my power against my own people? ...this is Enlil's kind of work!" (*Atra-Hasis*). Even so, Enlil forces Enki to take an oath and not interfere with the desolation of Man directly. Heeding his oath, Enki speaks "to the walls" of the king of Shuruppak claiming,

"Wall, listen to me! Reed hut, make sure you attend to all my words! Dismantle thy house, build a boat...roof it like Apsu so the sun [gods] cannot see inside it! Make upper decks and lower decks; the tackle must be very strong, the *bitumen* [tar] strong..."

(Found in varying texts,
such as the *Eridu Genesis, Epic of Gilgamesh, Atra-Hasis*)

By indirectly warning Mankind of the impending flood, Enki holds faithful in his oath to Enlil. However, Man is now aware of His impending doom. So forth that Ziusudra, king of Shuruppak (also known as *Atra-Hasis* or *Utanapishtim*; the man whom Enki indirectly warns), builds a boat and fills it with two of "every type of animal" along with his family.

Then the flood occurs.

For seven days and seven nights, the flood baptizes the earth of its wickedness. During this time, the gods have gone without food or water. In that their Human servants have been eradicated and therefore could not provide them with produce.

"Like sheep, [the gods] could only fill their windpipes with bleating;
Thirsty, as they were,
Their lips discharged only the rhyme of famine."

(*Atra*-Hasis)

After the seven days and seven nights, the flood subsides as Ziusudra emerges. In his gratefulness, Ziusudra makes an offering to the starving gods. "The hungry gods smell the fragrance and gather like flies over the offering..." (*Atra-Hasis*). Enki, not surprised at his creation's thoughtfulness (a quality of the gods), successfully persuades Enlil to be less harsh in dealing with Mankind for their noisiness. It is decided that Enki and Ninmah will force one out of every three women to not have successful births at the expense of the new class of temple priestesses (who could not bear children; evident by Sargon's mother).

However, this is merely the core of Sumerian mythology. There are many other intricate stories that help shape the testimony of Sumerian religion and ethics, such as the story of *"Man and His God"* (known also as the *Righteous Sufferer)* which was written over a **thousand years before** the Old Testament's *book of Job.* This ancient *wisdom* literature depicts the story of a righteous man who suffers ill-will from the "fate demon" in attempt to test the man's loyalty and faith with his god. The story's first line reads,

> "A person should steadfastly proclaim the exaltedness of His god."
>
> *(A Man and His God)*

This opening line emphasizes the general overtone of the *wisdom* offered by such literature. Considered to be the "Sumerian Job" many archaeologists claim this tale to be the basis of derivation for the biblical *book of Job.* For both doctrines carry resembling literary elements, though one exists thousands of years before the other. The literary parallels between all religious doctrines seem to be abundant throughout history. Evidenced by *Man and His God* which reads,

> "[God] eradicated the fate demon [who caused the young man's suffering] …[God] then turned the young man's suffering into joy. [God] set by him, as guardian, a benevolent protective demon... The young man steadfastly proclaims the exaltedness of his god... 'I have set my sights on you [my god] as on the rising sun...may you absolve my sin. May your heart be soothed towards me."
>
> *(Man and His God)*

Just as the opening line instructs, the wisdom-literature comes full circle in delivering its message. This story is written for the purpose of portraying the proper conduct for a victim's cruel or seemingly undeserved misfortune. Answering the day-old question of, "Why do bad things happen to good people?"

Another piece of religious Sumerian literature, which intends to give spiritual meaning, lie within *The Myth of Adapa*. In this tale, Adapa (representative of Mankind as the "first Apkallu king" or "first sage") is given divine *wisdom* from Enki (direct allegory towards Mankind's reception of "Me"). Created from the eternal Bread of Life and the eternal Water of Life, Adapa's existence is that of a "Mankind's representative" who is in charge of keeping and maintaining the fish supply (produce). In which Adapa's "word is now law." Once keenly aware of his newfound abilities, Man displays His irresponsibility with the godly powers. This is evident by Adapa irrationally cursing nature (South Wind) for flipping him over in his boat while maintaining the fish.

> "No sooner had [Mankind received the powers]
> That the South Wind's wing was broken;
> For seven days the South Wind did not blow towards the land."
> (*Myth of Adapa*)

Simply put, Adapa curses the South Wind (personified as a female) and His words (influenced by the godly powers of "Me") held enough earthly power to "physically break off the wing" of the South Wind. As in mortal Man carries to much emotion to wield divine omnipotence. This act infuriates the gods and especially Anu, god of wind and air. All-knowing in his own right, Anu asks, "...let someone bring him," for Adapa was to see trial before Anu for his actions. However, Enki, who created Mankind, feels the need to advise Adapa on how to properly behave in the presence of the gods.

> "They will show thee
> When thoust standest before Anu
> Food of Death they will present before thee. Eat not.
> Water of Death they will present before thee. Drink not.
> Garments they will set before thee, put them on.

Oil they will set before thee, anoint thyself.
The instructions I have given thee, forget not."
(*Myth of Adapa*)

Once Enki has successfully instructed mortal Man on how to behave in
the presence of the gods, Adapa is set before Anu. Questioning Adapa's lack
of responsibility, Anu hears his plead. In expressing his anger toward Adapa
he exclaims,

"Why does Enki disclose to impure Mankind
The heart of heaven [Anu] and earth [Ki]?
A heart has...made him a name?
What can we do with him? Fetch him the eternal bread of
life and let him eat!"
(*Myth of Adapa*)

Not knowing of Enki's predisposed instructions, Anu is fed up dealing
with Mankind. Questioning why Enki insists on making Man in their image,
Anu suddenly intends on allowing Adapa to eat from the eternal Bread of
Life and drink from the eternal Water of Life. In doing so, Anu will not have
to worry about the tedious tendencies of "mortal" Man. However, due to
Enki's advice, Adapa is obliged to refuse the offerings in thinking the act
of divine drinking or eating would kill him. By only accepting the divine
clothing and oil, Adapa (and thusly Mankind) is granted only a "portion" of
god-like abilities. For Mankind is gifted with the intellect and feelings of the
gods (by way of self-aware conscientiousness) yet are bound by the confines
of *time:* ineligible for immortality.

The fable in its entirety explains how Mankind (Adapa) is given the
divine powers of "Me" and is merely too emotionally ridden with subjectivity
to maintain full control of earth *without* the heed of heavenly guidance.

By comparing these mythological beliefs with the evidential reasoning
of objectivity, the origins of the Sumerian mythology (like most religions)
becomes very conclusive. In a most generalized way, the forces of chaos

battle the forces of order; in which *creation* emerges from the establishment of order. This theme is common amongst the core beliefs of all religions; the struggle between the god(s) and their *creation*. A struggle best represented by the departing of the child from the parent – the acceptance of the leaving of the nest and retrieving of independence.

It is by the bias word in which these beliefs are expressed – from the word of those "in contact with the gods" (any *ensi* for example*)*. These words entice the body of an ignorant population to bend to the intellectual whim of those in constant communication with the god(s) (who maintain order at the pleasurable expense of Man's servitude). It is within these natural events that bind all of the developing ancient civilizations together. Only does the geographic placement of these civilizations offer a difference in cultural development.

II. Ancient Egypt

History

Ignorance is not bliss.

Much like the people of *Mesopotamia* and the *Indus River Valley*, the early Egyptians thrived on the narrow seed-bed of its patron valley, the Nile River Valley. Like any original nomads who roam the plains of non-cultivated lands, the early Egyptians were indigenous wandering hunters and gatherers.

Unlike Mesopotamia, however, the ancient Egyptian civilization exists only on the banks of the Nile and nowhere outside of it due to the harsh climate of the African deserts. Be this as it may, the ambivalence of Egypt's aridness holds properties of both protection and isolation. This concept radically differs with the geography of Sumer, as the lands of the Levant expose their societies from all sides. As a result, the Sumerian perception and threat of death seem imminent, in which they retain an uncomplicated view of an afterlife or underworld (compared to the intricate view of the Egyptian perspective). For the vastness of the Egyptian desert acts as a natural barrier to exclude the outside world from interceding with its inhabitants' way of life.

By c. 5000 BCE (during the Ubaid period of Mesopotamia), groups of Egyptian wanderers had begun settling atop the fertile Nile Valley to eventually utilize agriculture. Due to the importance of agriculture, like all ancient civilizations, the sun officially becomes the most adorned object by these settlers. The sun provides warmth, light, and allows for the flourishment of crops (universal essentials for agriculture). Over two thousand years will pass as these isolated people master the development of ordered agricultural communities – undisturbed by any outside threat or influence.

Although this feat of isolation is true, a common belief amongst archae-ologists is asserting the idea of Egyptian hieroglyphs as possibly stemming from the Sumerian cuneiform script. Unlike the wedge-shaped writing style of cuneiform, Egyptian hieroglyphics are structured with more alphabetic elements and logographic representation. Whose logographs of pictorial quality usurp the quantitative representation of wedge iconography.

The isolation of Egypt dissolves as contact between the two ancient cultures takes place. Speculation points to the existence of contact (via trade) between the two civilizations as occurring during the Sumerian Uruk period (c. 3800 – 2900 BCE).

As previously covered, the earliest known cuneiform writings were found on clay tablets in Uruk, roughly three-and-a-half thousand years before the birth of Christianity. During the "Ubaid" period (contemporaneously for the Egyptians), the civilization is split between two factions: Upper and Lower Egypt. It is by the reverse-nature of the Nile's flow (which flows south to north) that cause Lower Egypt to reside in the north while Upper Egypt reigns in the south. A perceptive reciprocation of geographic locations.

Much like the neighboring Sumerians, the Egyptians start out as a non-unified region controlled by independent rulers. Resembling that of Mesopotamia, the Egyptians are able to successfully impose a class system. Unlike the Sumerians, however, the Egyptians retain a state of egalitarianism – relying not on "patriarchy" to influence gender seclusion, but on that of divine autocracy. These early Egyptians never had to worry about a transition between esteemed religious rulers (ensi) to some "big-Man" ruler (lugal). For the papacy of the pharaoh behaves as the god-king of the here and now. It is around this very time where a great cultural change occurs in Egypt, akin to the Sumerian reception of "Me" powers (perks of culture) in Uruk at the start of Mesopotamia's cultural birth.

By c. 3000 BCE, the ancient Egyptians document one of the earliest ancient hieroglyphic inscriptions depicting an early Egyptian king unifying Upper and Lower Egypt, known as the *Narmer Palette*. On this palette lay the earliest scribed depiction of Ra, the sun god of Egypt, in form of Horus the hawk. As the patron god of the authoritative city-state of Heliopolis, Ra begins asserting himself as head of the Egyptian pantheon (omnipresently resembling that of Anu from Uruk). One of their first documented deities, providing evidence of Egypt's rise in religious practice. Thus, one of the earliest documented forms of a unified religion and region *outside* of Sumerian culture. This unifying of the region introduces the dynastic kingdoms of Egypt.

Once a society transcends past the expression barrier they begin to express gratitude; feeling obligated to repay the Nature for its ever givingness. Why would Nature, and specifically these objects in the sky (i.e. the sun), be so compassionate towards Us? What have We had to offer these objects that would grant their display of benevolence?

This perception of gratitude stems from the omnibenevolent nature of the Nile. As discussed, the characteristics of Nature play a momentous role in defining the basis of comparison for each early civilization. Unlike the two rivers of Mesopotamia, the Nile's flooding cycle remain in such consistence that the early Egyptians are able to predict the river's flooding by simply studying the cosmic "rising" of Sirius – Our brightest star in the sky, marking the beginning of the new year. An early acknowledgment of astronomy, where the establishment of an Egyptian calendar could come to form; capturing the accuracy of the amount of days in a year (365, where the last five days are considered a blessing by the gods; extra days analogous to agricultural surplus). Along with this, the early Egyptians divide their year into three distinct seasons:

1. Akhet – the inundation (flooding) of the Nile (June – September)
   [Summer Solstice]

2. Peret – the plant/growth period (October – February)
   [Fall Equinox – Winter Solstice]

3. Shemu – the time of harvest (March – May)
   [Spring Equinox]

This consistency in seasonal prediction dismisses any unprecedented or random catastrophes to the early Egyptian settlers, accounting for the lack of intensive Levantine *"falling of Man*-like" events. Perhaps this is why the Egyptian culture remain practically unchanged for thousands of years to come.

Old Kingdom

Shortly after Egypt's unification brings a prosperous period known as the Old Kingdom (c. 2649 – 2153 BCE). During this period, the capital Memphis is established in the previously known Lower Egypt (north, towards the Nile Delta region). Unlike the *ensi* of Sumer, the pharaoh is perceived as an actual living god. Not just an intermediary between Mankind and His creators, but an actual living god of Our earthly realm. When the pharaoh dies, his grandiose spirit (known as *Ka*) would live on with vestigial omnipresence. These accolades of death were rationalized and deemed achievable through ritual practice: mummification, splurging of goods, and the implementation of incantations (burial prayers/hymns). These pharaonic beliefs inspire the Egyptians to create temples for their god-kings, much like the inspiration for the Sumerians to create their holy ziggurats. The ancient Egyptians construct royal "tombs" for their god-kings where their eternal spirit of *Ka* could reign supreme after death. Just as the Mesopotamian ziggurat houses the spirit of their cosmic gods, these royal tombs (exemplified through the Great Pyramids of Giza) house the spirits of every pharaonic king as an amalgamation of Horus in whole.

In order to import any outside goods (such as the limestone and ivory used in the construction of the Great Pyramids), the Egyptians had to learn to navigate the Nile via trade winds. As the Nile naturally flows south to north, the trade winds flow in the direction of inland Africa (north to south). Navigation of such magnitude becomes possible only through the teachings and trading with the Mesopotamians and their wind sails. Due to their superiority in technological advancements (especially bronze), the Sumerians are held in high esteem to the eyes of early Egyptians.

With their capital in the north, the pharaoh is better prepared to control the multi-regional trade and agriculture of Egypt and its surrounding lands. By c. 2200 BCE, the Old Kingdom begins to fade into political anarchy.

Possibly due to droughts, which occurs during the period of droughts that influence Sumer's demise (c. 2100 BCE), the Pharaoh begins to lose power in divine autocracy as other "worthy suitors" start to challenge the right to rule.

Which would make sense; if the pharaoh (god of earth) is in power during a time of natural calamity, his omnipotent influence can be called into question. Especially for a civilization who experience little-to-no cosmic infliction. This period of "weakening," known as the first intermediate period of ancient Egypt, causes the official ending of the Old Kingdom (c. 2649 – 2153 BCE).

Middle Kingdom

By c. 2060 BCE, a group of Nubian descent restore pharaonic rule in Egypt. This shift to Nubian rule introduces their patron god Amun, "replacing" Ra as the kingship is taken from Memphis to Thebes. After the collapse of the Old Kingdom subsides, the region once afflicted with disaster began to bear promise once more. By reclaiming old lands lost at the Old Kingdom's expense, the Middle Kingdom claims restoration by the reclaiming of agricultural and political dominance. As a result, the civilization's population, culture, and religion became revitalized.

This new divine kingship made efforts to democratize the religious experience for the common person. In which the Egyptian *afterlife* became open to any Human Being, granting anyone who possess a soul the opportunity to live after death *with* their gods. A dramatic shift from the strict traditions of the Old Kingdom.

There exists vast amount of trade during this period. The rulers of the Middle Kingdom are able to extend trade routes from the inlands of modern Sudan to the distant Mediterranean island of Cyprus (importing gold from the Nubian deserts and timber/cedar from the island of Cyprus). This extensive and multicultural trading system allows for the intermingling of many contemporary cultural views, including the already existing influence from Mesopotamia/Sumer. By trading with the Semitic world and beyond, the ancient Egyptians see no threat in allowing later Semites to migrate and live amongst themselves.

The last great ruler of the Middle Kingdom is Amenemhat III (c. 1860 – 1814 BCE). Although considered to have established a "golden age" for this period, Amenemhat III's actions cause for the downfall of the Middle Kingdom. Activity in mining and building endeavors (combined with severe flooding) cause for an economic decline. Also, in allowing Semitic-speaking settlers to work near the Nile delta, mass "Canaanite" descendants begin to destabilize the control over the delta region; inevitably leading to the collapse of Egypt once more.

By this point, a group of Sargon-like nomads conquer Egypt; the Semitic-speaking Hyksos. Considered by the Egyptians as "heka-khaswt" or "rulers of foreign lands" the Hyksos are of Canaanite/Phoenician descent. By utilizing their superiority in bronze weaponry, horse-bound chariots, and composite bows, the Hyksos relatively seize control over Egypt around c. 1720 BCE. Only to introduce the second intermediate period of Egypt's history.

New Kingdom

By c. 1560 BCE, a Theban prince named Ahmose I drives the Hyksos back into their foreign lands of Canaan (also known as **Palestine**). This ultimately launches the period of the New Kingdom (c. 1560 – 664 BCE). Being influenced by their previous Hyksos rulers introduces the New Kingdom Egyptians to new weaponry and tactics for battle, which succeeding rulers would utilize in driving the Hyksos out.

Nearly carried out by a single dynasty of pharaohs, the New Kingdom brings forth the emergence of Amun-Ra; a fusion of the old god Ra with that of the new god Amun. It is also within this period that the rulers of Egypt become definitively referred to as "Pharaoh" meaning "Great House" (housing their spirit of *Ka*; similar to Sumerian deification of ziggurats or "great houses"). Before this era, the "pharaohs" were held in regard as "priest-kings" in that the actual word "Pharaoh" had no empirical use – until this Egyptian New Kingdom.

Literacy had grown during the Middle Kingdom due to the allowance of lenience towards commoners. As a result, the majority of complete documentation thrives during the New Kingdom as more and more citizens became literate. The Egyptian writers of such an era characterize the times of Hyksos rule as "chaotic" and "destructive" with the intent of contrasting the New Kingdom's greatness with the "discontinuity" of that which came before it (an act later seen by the dichotomous teachings of the Roman Flavian dynasty against their former Julio-Claudia dynasty). Where Ahmose I become successful in reunifying Egypt by reestablishing divine kingship at Thebes.

Following his death, Ahmose's son Amenhotep I (c. 1526 – 1506 BCE) inherits and maintains a prosperous nation. Amenhotep I contributes greatly in the realm of arts and construction projects, as he becomes deified as "god of the artisans" of Deir el-Medina, an ancient village responsible for the master artistry done in the tombs of the Valley of Kings. It also is during this time that the famous *Book of the Dead* reaches its final form of accumulation – as the *Book of the Dead* is, in whole, a mere collection of many incantations (similar to that of Enheduanna's *Sumerian Temple Hymns*).

Amenhotep I is then led in succession by his son Thutmose I (c. 1506 – 1482 BCE). Immediately following his rise to power, Thutmose I goes on to broaden the scope of Egypt's rule. By extending Egyptian rule, the period of Thutmose I is met by a resolution of uprisings (evident by an uprising in Nubia) by keenly imposing the wrath of newfound Egyptian dominance in territories otherwise lost. So forth that he is able to pass down the throne to his son Thutmose II and eventually his daughter, Hatshepsut, who brings twenty of years of peace and prosperity to the Egyptian lands (resembling traits of Sumer's Gudea).

Hatshepsut (c. 1479 – 1458 BCE) is regarded as one of the most powerful rulers in Egyptian history. She retains divine kingship at the expense of her husband/half brother's death; the death of Thutmose II. Hatshepsut is responsible for more building projects than any other Pharaoh (excluding Ramesses II). Her projects carry such beauty and value that later successors attempt to claim them as their own, vandalizing her name from every monument. This occurs shortly after Hatshepsut's death, warranting blame towards a generational successor, more than likely her vengeful stepson/ nephew Thutmose III.

The immediate successor to Hatshepsut's throne is her stepson/nephew and rightful heir Thutmose III (c. 1479 – 1425 BCE), although not technically a successor, as he co-ruled with Hatshepsut for the first twenty years until her death. Once named Pharaoh, Thutmose III establishes what is now known as the Egyptian Empire – expanding their domain further and beyond ever before. To the extent that Thutmose III becomes credited with capturing over 350 cities outside of Egypt's previous control with over sixteen military campaigns in a twenty-year span. Much of this Pharaoh's reign is paid tribute through the vast amounts of surviving documentation (as Thutmose III is considered to be one of the best documented rulers, excluding Ramesses II). In doing so, archaeological speculation points to the act of defacing the history of Hatshepsut's reign would allow Thutmose III to absorb her twenty prosperous years, granting Thutmose III a more prominent legacy.

As expressed, much of the flourishment experienced by Egypt's New Kingdom comes to fruition at the hand of a single line of Pharaonic lineage. For example, it is Thutmose III's successor and son, Amenhotep II (c. 1425-1400 BCE), who bears the Pharaoh Thutmose IV (c. 1400 – 1390 BCE), credited for the *Dream Stele* that acknowledges him with the unearthing and remastering of the Great Sphinx. Only for Thutmose IV's son, Amenhotep III (c. 1386 – 1353 BCE) to become one of the most successful and prominent rulers in Egyptian history.

During Amenhotep III's rule, the New Kingdom of Egypt reaches a cultural, political, and economic zenith. The height of this divine kingship is expressed by the illustrious Temple of Luxor; one of the most complex monuments of Egyptian history. However, it was also during this time that a *religious cult* of worshippers for the god Amun began to develop enough wealth to challenge the Pharaoh's divine kingship. Due to this threat. Amenhotep III begins to identify with the sun god Aten in an attempt to wrest power from the cult of Amun. This ideology is passed down to his son Amenhotep IV who became so enthralled with the worship of Aten that he changes his name to Akhen**aten**; "of great use to [the god] Aten."

Akhenaten (c. 1353 – 1336 BCE) institutes one of history's first known forms of monotheism by abolishing Egypt's "old religion" in order to thwart the rising popularity of the cult of Amun. By instituting monotheism, the worship and adornment of Aten (the true "one and only" god) brings a period of religious shift. Influenced in naming his son Tutankh**aten,** the young heir inherits a nation before the age of nine years. A young ruler who inevitably restores the values and culture of Egypt's "old religion." Upon his father's death, it is speculated that the powerful influence of the cult of Amun "convince" the young Tutankh**aten** to overturn the heretical monotheistic values instilled by his father. So forth that the young Pharaoh changes his name to Tutankh**amun**, who "rules" for a short span from c. 1336 – 1327 BCE.

At this point, the influence of Amun's cult is obvious. For the reign of Tutankhamun (who rules young and just as well dies young) is given to a general by the name of Horemheb (c. 1320 – 1295 BCE), who adamantly sought to erase Akhenaten from Egypt's history. Horemheb, for all intents and purposes, is generally known as an "old-school" general who held strong "old-school" beliefs. Therefore, it is Horemheb who is generally accredited with restoring Egypt back to its classic polytheistic ways. It is at this point the New Kingdom pharaonic line of succession broke from its blood-bound ties: where military succession overtook the throne (much like the Sumerian passing of power from *ensi* to *lugal*). Horemheb then dies and passes the throne to another general in Ramesses I who eventually gives the title of divine kingship to Egypt's most notable Pharaoh: Ramesses II (c. 1279 – 1213 BCE).

Ramesses II is often referred to as the nameless Pharaoh of the Hebrew oppression during the biblical Exodus. Be this as it may, no form of evidence holds this statement to its claim. Ramesses II left an extraordinary legacy in regaining old lands and commissioning more monuments and scripts than any other Pharaoh in history. Yet, through all of this, not once are the "Hebrews" or "Israelites" mentioned in any doctrine.

Ramesses II would be challenged by the nomadic, yet prominent, Hittite Empire who have already conquered the Babylonians. By "defeating" the Hittites at the Battle of Kadesh (c. 1274 BCE), Ramesses II signs the world's first peace treaty with the Hittite king. By the end of Ramesses II's rule, he moves the nation's capital out from Thebes – subsequently losing favor with Amun and his cult. The void of kingship in Thebes allows for the cult of Amun to rise again and re-challenge Pharaonic kingship. With the line Ramesses' kingship ruling Lower Egypt, the cult of Amun is able to reclaim political growth in Thebes of Upper Egypt. The priesthood of Amun are able to accumulate so much power by establishing the Sumerian-like "intermediary" position between Man and Amun. By having an intermediary with god (Amun: the one who sustains balance in the Universe), the priesthood can intercede on the people's behalf, diminishing the role of the Pharaoh. No longer is the ruler seen as an earthly-bound god but as a subordinate of Amun. Subject only to the will of Amun's word; spoken from the tongue of the cult itself. Spoken from the will of mortal Man. The king was no longer a god, for god himself became the king. Once Amun gains the recognition as true king, the political power of the Pharaoh is transferred to Amun's priesthood. This shift in power brings Egypt to a period of decadence that would ultimately lead to its cultural demise.

Religion

The <u>human condition</u> is a unified trait of Our species.

Recurring similarities in religious and cultural development gives evidence to Mankind's uniformity in consciousness. Much like the Sumerians in their collective linear thought process of unintentional introspection, the Egyptians acknowledge innate characteristics through the similar mechanism of deifying and anthropomorphizing; by assigning characteristics or "roles" for the unexplained phenomena of Nature. Egyptian and Sumerian intuitors unknowingly began to unravel a rationale for introspection. An introspective shift, which compels Mankind to transition His once primitive ideals of "cosmic God(s)" through a conventional comprehension of Nature. Where the intention of cosmology (and thusly religion) is to familiarize the unknown. To acknowledge the vast uncertainties of the Universe through the subjective extrapolation of One's own experiences.

A paradigm shift of arrogance. Where, commonly enough, Man deifies Nature in concordance with His own Human characteristics. An instinctual response to Our lingering ignorance. For the Egyptians, like all ancient intuitors, create god(s) in the image of themselves.

The ancient Egyptians believe that Life (and therefore Mankind) exists as some slight segment of some eternal journey. This eternal odyssey is orchestrated by the forces of Nature (who take deified form). The goal in Life is to uphold and maintain "*ma'at*" or "harmony" in that the actions of One directly affecting the consequences of the whole. Where the microcosmic pieces of a macrocosmic whole affect the totality of collective harmony. For Mankind's destiny, like all Life, is to attain everlasting bliss. This idea of harmonic *ma'at* compels the individual to invest towards the greater good and not their independent self, emphasizing the importance of Life's unity in uniformity. Emphasizing the superiority of objectivity over individual subjectivity. By honoring the principle of *ma'at* and living a life of social dependence, One becomes aligned with the gods upon death; becoming eligible for a spiritual afterlife or "mirror-world" of One's life on earth. This "becoming aligned with the gods" is similar to the Sumerian idea of Mankind's reception of "Me" in that the gods relish in allowing Mankind to be representing their godly qualities. All in all, One must live their life with compassion and unity for their fellow sentient beings in order to enjoy the splendors of their eternal journey after death.

This "journey" begins with the creation of existence out of the swirling waters of chaos known as "Nu" (similar to the Sumerian primordial waters of Apsu). From this chaos rose the primordial "hill" known as Ben-Ben (mountainous representation of Our physical Universe). Upon the great hill stood the god of creation, Atum (associated with the sun god Ra), who creates himself from the chaotic waters of Nu. The title differentiation between "Atum" and "Ra" (or the later given name "Khnum") is to give meaning between the observable sun's position throughout a day. To the extent that Ra would rise and shine on the mounds of Ben-Ben, only for Atum to take back his original form at the day's end. From a parthenogenesis standpoint (a natural form of asexual reproduction; as demonstrated by Atum/Ra), the self-creation of Atum himself is directly analogous to an eternal cycle of creation and chaos (Life and death). Where in some traditions (like the Greeks in their myth of the Phoenix) Atum takes form of a <u>snake;</u> the animal known for "renewing itself every morning" by the shedding of its form. At the end of a creation cycle, Atum will return to the primordial watery chaos without form. Only to be reborn again as Ra in his glory.

In recognizing his loneliness, Atum mates with his own shadow in the "spitting out" of Shu, god of air, and Tefnut, goddess of moisture. Shu, as a *physical* feat, establishes the basic principles of Life, which includes everything in physical existence (matter; atoms, plants, animals, etc.). All while Tefnut, in *spiritual* form, establishes the principles of order; binding the laws of Nature in establishing *ma'at*. By doing so, the two leave their father by himself on the hill of Ben-Ben. Worried, Atum sends out his Eye of Ra (also known as the "Udjat Eye") to search for his children. Upon their return, Shu and Tefnut rejoin with their father who sheds tears of joy.

Consequently enough, these tears of joy inevitably give birth to Mankind and His likeliness with the gods; only for Shu and Tefnut to create "Geb" (earth) and "Nut" (sky-heavens) (similar to Tiamat creating Anshar and Kishar, who create Anu and Ki) for Mankind to thrive. Geb and Nut, though brother and sister, fall madly in love (represented by their "oneness" like *anu-ki*). This incestual affair is not approved by Atum who separates the two, creating the distinction between the heavens and the earth (compare Enlil separating *anu-ki*). Be this as it may, Geb has already impregnated Nut – who gives birth to **four** of the **seven** fate decreeing gods of Egypt; Osiris, Isis, Set, and Nephthys. The seven gods in total are:

1. Ra – (macrocosmic) god of the sun

2. Isis – queen of the gods

3. Hathor – goddess of love and beauty

4. Osiris – god of *wisdom* and justice

5. Set – the god of *evil*

6. Nephthys – protectress of the dead

7. Horus, the Young – (microcosmic) god of the sun

Once the order of the Universe is established, the third manifestation of Atum (named Khnum) creates Life. Khnum, god of creation and rebirth, molds Life out of clay to give it form (much like Enki when assisting in the Creation of Man). Understand, as previously mentioned, that the perception of the observable sun's positioning exploits "which god the sun" is being represented at each given position. Therefore, the god Atum can be "interchanged" with the title of Ra or Khnum, as they all represent the sun in totality (similar to the likeliness of the Father, the Son, and the Holy Spirit). A trinity of naming and renaming. With this being said, and once Khnum brings forth creatures, the perceived "tears of Ra" can then parallel the reoccurring theme of an affliction Mankind receives from His gods (powers of Me; fruit of knowledge). Once Mankind becomes distinguished, He then makes a covenant with the gods; divine protection in exchange for the maintenance of *ma'at*.

From the gods, Osiris is chosen by Atum to co-rule the earth with his sister Isis. In doing so, Osiris creates the land of Egypt in perfection with the Nile River to provide the needs of Mankind. Osiris acts in accordance to *ma'at*, honoring his pantheon by keeping all things (including Mankind and His gods) in harmonious balance. All the while Set and Nephthys are coupled to rule the netherworld.

Set begins to grow envious of his brother's glory and power on earth, so he establishes an elaborate plot to dethrone Osiris. In creating a detailed chest specifically for Osiris, Set throws a great banquet in his honor. At the end of the event, Set offers a "great-chest" to Osiris who "best fits inside." A suspicious Osiris tests this claim only for Set to lock him in and dispose of said chest afloat the Nile. As a result, Set tells the rest of the gods that Osiris has died; establishing Set as the new ruler of earth. This corrupt act by Set disrupts the balance of *ma'at*.

Isis does not believe in Set's lies and so decides to go searching for Osiris with the help of her sister Nephthys. In searching, the two find the chest inside of a *tree* at the city of Byblos. Isis then blesses the people of this city for helping her retrieve the chest (representing the importance of the city of Byblos (Canaan), who fund the Egyptians with *papyrus*; an important import for the Egyptian revolution in documentation). Isis then brings the body of Osiris back to Egypt in attempt to bring him back to life. Needing to find Osiris's missing piece, Isis then instructs Nephthys to watch over the body until she returns.

Set becomes worried in thinking Osiris might be found. Only then does Set notice that his wife/sister is gone. Confused at her disappearance, he later asks Nephthys of her previous whereabouts upon her return. By seeing through her attempt at lying, Set extracts the whereabouts of Osiris's body from Nephthys. As he discovers the body of Osiris, Set shreds the body into forty-two pieces and scatters the remains throughout Egypt (symbolizing the forty-two nomes of ancient Egypt). When Isis returns, she discovers what Set has done and weeps at the second loss of her husband/brother. Nephthys, feeling guilty, offers to help Isis by assisting in finding all of Osiris's pieces. Wherever the two find a piece, they would bury it as a shrine for Osiris would arise to protect each "piece" (representing a city) from Set. In this way, the historic forty-two provisions of ancient Egypt are taken into account. Once they've assembled Osiris in his entirety, Isis realizes they are still missing a piece – his reproductive organ. A piece which had been eaten by a *fish*, forcing Isis to create a replacement/artificial phallus. Knowing he would never be complete again, Isis mates with Osiris in an attempt to preserve his earthly kingship by heir. This act brings forth the first earthly king named Horus (which is the secret name of Ra). Once this act is complete, the incomplete Osiris descends into the underworld to replace Set as the "righteous judge of the netherworld."

Horus "The Younger" is then raised in secret from Set, until he is of age to challenge Set's kingship. Once of age, Horus and Set battle until Horus claims victor; banishing Set from Egypt to wander the desert for eternity (analogous to the story of Cain and Abel). As the new ruler of earth, Horus reigns supreme in restoring *ma'at*. Horus, who would rise every morning, is credited with bringing light and unity to the heavens and the earth. Where, like Enlil, the son of the heavenly king retains kingship in response to the splitting of the heavens and the earth.

And so is the core of Egyptian religion. Once the sun had *set* at night, Man can only have **faith** that it will rise again. Therefore, early Egyptians depend on the rationale of their belief system (at that time). The rationale of the "Argument of Ignorance." As Horus and Set represent the oldest and most proverbial dualities in Mankind's history: Good vs. Evil.

As a result of recognizing patterns through the qualities of their surroundings, Ancient Egyptians anthropomorphize their perception of the human condition respectively. Through the use of hieroglyphics, the Ancient Egyptians are able to document and express the perception they held for their adorned gods of Nature who represent the core principles of what it means to be Human. Evidence of Our natural yearning to learn, innately following the same developmental structure as other early civilizations (such as Mesopotamia). The use of anthropomorphizing is significant in understanding the true nature of the <u>human condition</u>. A testament to coping with the ignorance of this condition by relating innate Human intuition with the thoughts and feelings of appropriate personified entities. For example, adorning the sun and personifying the sun as a creature of "sky reaching" abilities, such as a bird of sorts (falcon or hawk). As Horus was personified as such.

The early Human Beings of Ancient Egypt held **faith** in the divinity of Nature itself. Between the four major cities of Egypt, which consists of Hermopolis, Heliopolis, Memphis, and Thebes, each believed in various accounts of creation called *cosmogenesis*. Much like the Abrahamic religions of Christianity, Islam, and Judaism, these various accounts of creation represent competing theologies (more explicitly related to the core beliefs of neighboring Sumer). However, the heliopathic myth of creation carries high influence, as the ancient city of Heliopolis (translating as the "city of the sun") is known to be Egypt's affluent religious center.

In essence, the Ancient Egyptians conceive the notion that the cycle of creation and destruction are inevitable. As if Our ailment of evil needs to be purified every so often as a result of itself.

Sound familiar?

This universal ideology is the basis for which the Egyptians perceive their cycle of Life. Which accounts for the "timeline of time" to expose the mortality of Ourselves. Just as the old die, new Life will emerge. The constant bout between Life and death.

Life and death. Good and evil.

A strong distinction between the beliefs of ancient Sumer and the Egyptians stem from the core ideology of Life after death. For the Sumerians see little extravagance in Life after death as death loomed imminent. Yet, the Egyptians were not as exposed to an impending death based on their geographic isolation. In which the Egyptians develop a better appreciation for Life. So forth that they embody what it means to live beyond death. That the body may perish, but the soul, as the consciousness, continues on. Upon death, the individual is presented at the Hall of Truth before Osiris and Anubis ("guider of souls"). The heart (soul) is then weighed on a golden scale against the "white feather of *ma'at*." If the heart is lighter than the feather, then the soul is considered "pure" and allowed into the "Field of Reeds" (heaven) – a place of purification and eternal bliss that mirrors Our experience on earth. However, if the heart is heavier than the feather of *ma'at,* then the heart is dropped on the floor and devoured by Ammit, the devourer of souls, where the soul then ceases to exist.

This ceasing of the soul's existence is not the same as the biblical "hell." The Egyptians did not need for an eternal state of damnation, as the state of eternal darkness/nothingness instilled fear enough. To them, a state of unconsciousness as nothingness (which occurs at the devouring of One's soul) contradicts the order of *ma'at*. Existence, which is a part of "the journey" of *ma'at,* is a natural state of One's consciousness. To exist is to still be apart of the overall harmony of Life, both good and bad. Therefore, "not existing" becomes more terrifying than an eternal state of torment; for existence is still present in the experience of such damnation. To make up for the natural presence of *evil,* the ancient Egyptians dismiss of the notion of omnibenevolence by simply deifying *evil* outright in the form of a corrupt-seeking god, Set, who parallels Catholicism's *Lucifer, the fallen angel.*

The uniqueness of religious testimony lay not within a specific religion itself, but within the distinct manifestation of what it means to be a Human Being. Ultimately a script in articulating the nature of Our human condition. There holds an abundance of similarities between supposed organic knowledge and irrefutable objection. Truth in the origins of the Sumerian religion, Egyptian religion, the Abrahamic religions, Greek and Roman mythology, Buddhism, Hinduism, etc. This idea of spiritual apprehension stems directly from the source of its creation – Us; Human Beings themselves. Just as the instinct of a spider to spin a web, where the creation of the web itself is not an ability designated to any spider in particular, but an ability given to the species of arachnids. A common trait as a result of evolutionary phenomena. A coping mechanism to entangle its prey for survival. As is religion: a coping mechanism for Our species to further understand and appease to the ignorance of Our human condition. For there are far too many commonalities within the development of opposing religions and cultures to expose these truths as isolated incidents. The evidence becomes very conclusive, where the forces of chaos battle the forces of order; in which *creation* emerges from the establishment of order out of chaos. The common motif of a struggle between the god(s) and their *creation:* Mankind.

Only in the difference of experiencing Life does the truth vary. It is by the bias word in which these beliefs are exposed to those lost in ignorance – the word of those "in contact with the gods" (ensi, Pharaoh, Rabbi, Magi, Bishop, priest, etc.). These words entice the **body of the population** (illiterate farmers/workers) to bend to the whim of those who maintain order with their gods and livelihood; but only at the pleasurable expense of the peoples' servitude. It is within the natural events of introspection which binds all of the developing ancient civilizations together. For only in the geographic placement of a civilization does any difference in cultural development occur.

III. Judaism – The Chosen People

History

The history of the Hebrew people is very convoluted.

Whose history is foretold by the scripture of the Hebrew Bible (known as the Tanakh), which claims historical accuracy. Fault in acknowledging this doctrine as a piece of objective testimony lies within the doctrine itself. However, by cross-referencing extraneous historical testimonies, One begins to understand the objective origins of the "chosen people."

The holy land of Canaan (later known as Palestine; sought out by the biblical prophet Abram) originates with the universal cultural development process in its occupants adopting the agrarian lifestyle. This region of the Middle East holds extreme significance in terms of its geography; so forth that the land is still fought over to this day. Located on the western banks of the Mediterranean Sea, the coastal Levant connects many trade routes between many different civilizations – such as Mesopotamia, ancient Egypt, the Asia Minor (Hittites/Lydians), etc.

The early Semitic settlers of the eastern Mediterranean slowly develop into a thriving region with emerging civilizations; one of them being the renowned Byblos, established c. 2600 BCE. This import city becomes known as the leading trade hub of the Semitic world, namely for their papyrus exchange with the Egyptians. The very name of this city is later coined by the Greeks as *biblia,* which derives its meaning in describing the papyrus-books distinct to Byblos. It was also in this very city where the alphabet began its evolution. The widespread cuneiform offered by the Sumerians is used as a platform to further create a new-and-improved alphabet that would further be improved on by the Greeks and Romans. Soon thereafter, other cities and civilizations began to compete with Byblos in terms of importance relative to the overall geographic advantages Canaan (Palestine) has to offer. One of these competing groups are the esteemed Phoenicians.

The Phoenicians are renowned intuitors who are crucial in assisting with the evolution of the alphabet; well known for their practicality and ingenuity. By the end of the third millennium BCE, the Phoenicians establish prominent cities of their own in Tyre and Sidon. These Semitic people are proficient in engineering, astronomy, and most of all navigation (all which stem from original Mesopotamian/Egyptian influence). The language and alphabet of these ancient people directly resemble the ancient Hebrew language-to-come.

Ancient Canaan's geographic placement offers one of the world's first direct districts of multicultural diffusion: resulting from societal intermingling via <u>trade</u>. It is within this enticing quality alone that distinguishes this land from many others of ancient times. So forth that foreign rule becomes of the norm; in which outside settlers would come to Canaan (Palestine) for conquest. The constant routine of conquest and appeasement result in the decline of the region's <u>fertility</u> over *time*. Where, due to the land being artificially terraformed, the sedimentary foundation of the land begins to dry up – losing its fertility. These periods of over-use cause for the occurring calamities in the region's history.

Thought to have occurred around c. 2000 BCE, it is argued that a group of nomads from either Ur (as known as the Chaldeans) or Şanlıurfa (also known as the city of Urfa or "Edessa" to the Greeks) leave their homeland in search of new pastures. Remember, it is also around this time in the year c. 2004 BCE when Ur is conquered by the neighboring Elamites and Amorites. A period of distraught that acknowledges the plunging of all Mesopotamia into a "dark age" and thus a need to leave the lands. This migrate venture symbolically represents the eventual establishment of the later known tribes of the Levant including those of Israel. This gradual reformation of the region forces its indigenous people out. Most of these refuges are Canaanites (Palestinians), who flee to Egypt's Nile Delta region during their Middle Kingdom. The Egyptians would have allowed this influx in immigrants due to their standing relationship with the Canaanites via trade. However, around

c. 1600 BCE, another drought is thought to have curse the land of Canaan (Palestine) that would result in the fleeing of even more Palestinians from their homelands. This drought, and many others like it, is likely caused by the non-stop-usage of the indigenous lands after the agricultural revolution. In which this biblical "plague" is caused by either the conquering Hittites of the north, who gain prominence shortly before, or more probably by the drought that would have brought starvation to the region's inhabitants. Either way, some are forced to flee north towards modern Turkey (to Haran for example, which neighbors the city of Urfa) while others fled south towards Egypt. This abandoning of the Levant leaves the region exposed to the open floodgates of any nomadic conquerors – including the impending Hittites and Assyrians.

Those who fled to take refuge in Lower Egypt establish their own means of "sub-civilizations" within Egyptian jurisdiction by cultivating the fertile Nile Delta – depending not entirely on the Egyptians directly to survive. These groups of Semitic immigrants eventually see yet another influx in population brought forth by the plague-based afflictions of their homeland. Eventually these Semitic refugees form alliance in reuniting to become the known Hyksos of Egypt's Second Intermediate period and establish their own capital city in Lower Egypt named Avaris. The core justification in explaining the Hyksos "out-of-nowhere" rise is found in their profound technological superiority over the Egyptians. These attributes include the use of bronze weaponry (adopted from Sumerians), advanced military tactics involving hours-bound chariots, and proficiency with the composite bow. Before all of this, the Egyptians had remained in blissful isolation from the provisions of the outside world – bearing no necessity to evolve militarily. Resulting in their inferiority when at the mercy of the advanced Hyksos and the inevitable end of the Egyptian Middle Kingdom.

The term *Hyksos* originates from the Egyptian phrase *"heka-khaswt"* meaning "rulers of foreign countries" (as previously covered). Meaning these Semitic Hyksos are not a "new" group of inhabitants to Egypt, as this label only proposes such a title once in power. It appears that the Hyksos spare relatively most of Egypt untouched, displaying either their profound respect towards the Egyptians for allowing their civil entry or by means of sheer inability. Within fifty years of establishing their capital city, the Hyksos conquer the old capital of Memphis. This rise of power by the Hyksos brings an immediate splitting of the Egyptian region once more between the north (Lower) and the south (Upper). These rulers of the north were not oppressive to the Egyptian culture, rather they embrace it (much like their Sargonic ancestors). So forth that the fifth ruler of the Hyksos Empire, Apophis (c. 1580 – 1550 BCE), commissions the recopy of thousands of ancient Egyptian texts at Heliopolis and Memphis. Not only this, but the adoration for the devilish god Set began its due diligence.

That is until the Egyptian savior of the New Kingdom succeeds as Pharaoh: Ahmose I (c. 1539 – 1514 BCE). Ahmose (also known to the Greeks as Ahmosis or "child of the Moon [God]") observes and adopts the advanced military tactics of the Hyksos and is eventually capable of standing up to them. Halfway through his twenty-five-year reign, Ahmosis I begins to launch attacks on the Hyksos in an attempt to reclaim the lands of northern Egypt. He is successful in reclaiming Heliopolis and eventually expelling the Hyksos from Egypt entirely. However, this was no easy task. For it took Ahmosis four different attempts in attacking the Hyksos capital of Avaris before he was finally able to conquer the city. Exemplifying the awe-encompassing power of the Hyksos. With this being said, modern archaeological surveys of southern Canaan (Palestine) and northern Egypt determine that Ahmosis intended only to expel the power of the Hyksos and no more. Evidence for such a claim retain authenticity by the Egyptian's decision to only destroy the Hyksos cities rather to rebuild atop their ruins – something a conquest-bent Pharaoh would have likely done in forcing retribution.

For the objection of history concludes a Semitic mass exodus from Egypt by the hands of a Moses.

There is much objective evidence lacking in telling the affairs of what occurred after the Hyksos' expulsion. Yet, much has been documented in relaying the course of events preceding their departure. By piecing these events together, it appears that the Egyptians understood the effectiveness of the Hyksos in combat and saw the futility in the further pursuit of their total demise. In which the Hyksos mass exodus from Egypt, led and enforced by Ahmosis I, is met without quarrel upon their defeat. To such an extent that the Hyksos, now without a homeland but still militarily capable, attempt to reclaim their lands of over a century ago. Only for Ahmosis' brother and successor, Kamose (c. 1555 – 1550 BCE) to later refer to the Hyksos king Apophis as "chieftain of Retjenu" or "ruler of Canaan (Palestine)."

No longer "rulers of foreign countries" the Hyksos retain their ethnic title as Semitic semi-nomads. The Egyptians refer to them later as *shasu* meaning "those who are on foot." Wandering back to their homelands, these *shasu* nomads return to the Levant; only there are they met by the powers that be (the Hittites, Neo-Canaanites, and Assyrians). Fighting to reclaim their country of origin, the still-proficient "former Hyksos" become successful in the reclaiming of lands in the Levant. These reclaiming of lands are then divided amongst "the tribes of shasu" who are only made mention in Egyptian texts during post-Hyksos rule (during the reign of Amenhotep III). It is at the temple at Soleb, dedicated to Amun-Ra and constructed by Amenhotep III, which contains a topographical list (regional list) of tribes located in the Levant during his rule. These tribes are named "the shasu of X" in which the variable 'X' holds placement value (mathematically based). Many biblical historians claim a parallel from these "tribes of shasu" to the "first six judges" or "twelve tribes of Israel" in their distinct characteristics, as the Egyptians never make mention of "Israelite" or "Hebrew" tribes. Where the entirety of these shasu tribes are unified under the idolatry of the vindictive, warlike god known as *Yahweh* (a redaction of the Babylonian Marduk who reigns supreme as the Levantine god during this very period). This is made evident by many Egyptian New Kingdom inscriptions of "*t3 sh3sw ya-h-wa*" meaning "the shasu of YHW" (*YHW* or *Yahweh*).

Another New Kingdom scripture, which bears an evidential comparison connecting the "shasu" with the "chosen" Hebrew people, lay within the biblical relationship between the Hittites and the descendants of Abram. The Hittites, known previously as the conquerors of Hammurabi's Babylonia, were not of "one people" like the Egyptians but an amalgamation of many people.

Like their predecessors (which the Babylonians are of Amorite/Akkadian/ Sumerian descent), the Hittites conquer the Babylonians and merely adopt the best aspects of the conquered culture and force the populous to appease or perish. Thus, furthering cultural diversity and "ethnic" blending.

This empire grew not from a superior ethnic conquest but from the culmination of assimilation and superior technology (that being iron). The Hittites are accredited as being the first civilization to utilize iron effectively in substitution for bronze. In such a manner that would allow the Hittites to flourish in prominence in the lands of the Middle East during the middle of the second millennium BCE. The Tanakh/Old Testament claims these ancient Hittites as inevitable adversaries of the Hebrews; yet expose an intimate hypergamic relationship between the two. As Genesis 26:34 reads,

> "Esau (son of Isaac; grandson of Abram) took to wife [both] Judith the daughter of Beeri the Hittite, and Bashemath the daughter of Elon the Hittite."

Representing a mutuality between the prominent Hittites and the tribal Hebrews (shasu). This mutual relationship is further exemplified during the Battle of Kadesh (c. 1274 – 1269 BCE) between the Egyptians (led by Ramesses II) and the Hittites. This battle is the product of the Hittites conquering Egyptian vessel states during their expansion: such as Byblos and areas of Syria (namely Ugarit and Kadesh). The Egyptians, not taking kindly to these acts, engage with the Hittites in great battle at Kadesh, an important city of Syria. Though the new-and-improved efficiency of the Egyptian military prove formidable against contemporary technology, they are outmatched by the iron-wielding Hittites. Ultimately both sides surrender in signing Mankind's first peace treaty in the *Peace Treaty of Kadesh* c. 1269 BCE. It is within the Egyptian account of this battle that claims the Hittites as being allied by the Semitic "shasu tribes" relaying the assertion of a mutual Hittite-Hebrew relationship.

The Battle of Kadesh weakens both the Egyptians and Hittites to the core of their civilization's stability. The demise of the Egyptian civilization would be delayed by the grace of their seclusive geography. However, the Hittites would soon fall after the historic battle and signing of the peace treaty. By c. 1200 BCE arising tribes (such as the Lydians along with coastal sea-raiders; known as the biblical Philistines) conquer the Hittites of the north and remove their conceptual "central power." Without the Hittites to impose their iron fist, smaller nations (like the Israelites) are then able to experience a period of independence. This period of antiquity unites the former "tribes of shasu" under a Hebrew kingdom of Israel.

But who unites these tribes?

Biblically speaking (from Joshua to Samuel to Saul to David to Solomon) there remains historical speculation to question the integrity of the question's answer. Yet there exists enough archaeological evidence for the acute acknowledgement of David and Solomon's reign from the first millennium BCE. Where Joshua and Samuel may simply represent the original wandering tribes of shasu until a more peaceful period (represented through Saul) establishes the organization in unifying the Semitic tribes. Only for David and his son Solomon to inevitably assure the sanctity of the Hebrew Kingdom. These "twelve tribes of Israel (shasu)" are similar to the independent city-states of ancient Sumer, except these tribes are united under the single god Yahweh by a guiding set of laws that will later be acknowledged as the *Ten Commandments*.

David's son Solomon ultimately causes the kingdoms unravel. Solomon (c. 970 – 931 BCE) is scribed as the third monarch of a unified Israel and is well known for his ostentatious lifestyle of lavish living and extensive expenditures – most notably the renowned Temple of Jerusalem. During his reign, Solomon creates a semi-bureaucratic state consisting of twelve districts or "tribes." In doing so, he establishes Israelite colonies to the north while one tribe in Judah remain the "capital tribe" of the south with its capital at Jerusalem. Judah, considered to be the "true" tribe of the Israelites, retains individual privileges that alienates the other tribes in causing internal turmoil. These civil disputes cause conviction for the northern tribes in becoming susceptible to the "false-idolatry" of their alien neighbors. Additionally, by embarking on such an expensive campaign, Solomon is forced to impose heavy taxes and radical changes to the overall diplomacy of his kingdom. Only after the death of Solomon does the splitting of the "shasu tribes" take place between the Israelites of the north and the tribe of Judah in the south. Judah holds the legacy of Solomon with its capital holy city in Jerusalem while the Israelites designate their holy capital at Samaria. The ultimate result of Solomon's kingship is scarred by the severance of unification in the "loss of the Ten Tribes of Israel" as "a result of Solomon's greed." This split has enormous implications on the lasting religious and cultural values of the now-divided Hebrew people. In such a manner that the civil disunity creates a religious partite between the Israelites and Judahites, where the Israelites claim divinity through "Elohim" and the Judahites retain divinity through "Yahweh." The symbolic account for this severance is foretold many times throughout the Old Testament. Once by the story of Esau (Judah) and Jacob (Israel), told from the perspective of northern Elohists. Another by the tale Moses' descent from Mount Sinai in discovering "his people" false worshipping an idol other than Yahweh, told from the perspective of the southern Judahites.

These two Jewish kingdoms remain in disorderly existence until the conquest of the Assyrian Empire. The conquest of the Assyrians is so hated by chroniclers of the Tanakh/Old Testament, claiming these foes to be "as brutal and violent as they were numerous." Under their first major king, Sargon II, the Assyrians conquer the northern kingdom of Israel by laying siege on the Israeli capital of Samaria in c. 722 BCE – reinforcing the notion of conquest under appeasement. This conquest enforces the deportation of roughly thirty-thousand Israelites from the north who take refuge throughout the Fertile Crescent; including their "second-Jewish-state" of southern Judah. This mass increase of Israelites to Judah brings with them their distinct "Elohistic" religious ideals; which began influencing the divinity of Yahweh.

Then the thirteenth king of Judah Hezekiah comes to power and quickly begins purifying the divinity of Yahweh by enforcing an outlaw of traditions and followings to outside religions. This purging of false idols becomes the first imposition of *monotheism* since Egypt's Akhenaten.

The overall internal struggle amongst the Hebrews proves wasteful due to the impending invasion of the Assyrians. In the end, the Assyrians ravage through Judah by destroying forty-six of its cities. In enforcing this dominance, the Assyrians put to focus the besieging of Jerusalem in c. 701 BCE.

This is where the biblical scripture starts to expose obvious illegitimacy in historical accuracy. For the most part, the chronology of Abrahamic events preserves a historical reminiscence. However, every once in a while, the words of the "original" scripture expose themselves with obvious evidence of testimonial bias and discontinuity. For example, objective testimony of the invasion of Judah (from the Assyrians, Hebrews, and later Greeks) claim historical similarities only in these facts: the destruction of forty-six Judahite cities, the "sparing of Jerusalem," and the notion of Hezekiah paying harsh tribute toward the Assyrian king Sennacherib. The Assyrian account (along with later accounts such from Herodotus) boast of the Assyrian king as shutting Hezekiah and his people in Jerusalem: surrounding them "like a caged bird." Where the Assyrians, who are known for terrorizing those who resist, force the king of Judah to face extortion via tribute or perish in the total conquest of Judah. Although accurate in the "sparing" of Jerusalem, the biblical scripture claims the true reason behind the city's pardoning, stating,

> "[Sennacherib] will not enter [Jerusalem] or shoot an arrow here. He will not come before it with shield or build a siege ramp against it...'He will not enter this city,' claims the Lord. 'I will defend this city and save it, for my sake and for the sake of David [and his descendants].' That night, the angel of Death went out and put to death a hundred and eighty-five thousand in the Assyrian camp. When all the people got up the next morning – they were all the dead bodies! So, king Sennacherib broke camp and withdrew. He returned to Nineveh and stayed there."
>
> (II Kings 19: 31-36)

The Hebrew account depends on the divine interaction of their god Yahweh to directly prevent Assyrian dominion. Even though this notion is expressed, the biblical scripture still somehow allocates for the factor of Judah paying massive tribute.

> "Now in the fourteenth year of King Hezekiah, Sennacherib came up against all the fortified cities of Judah and seized them. Then Hezekiah sent to the king of Assyria in Lachish, saying, 'I have done wrong [in revolting against your will]. Withdraw from me; whatever you impose on me I will bear.' So, the king of Assyria required of Hezekiah three hundred talents of silver and thirty talents of gold. Hezekiah gave him all the silver which was found in the house of the Lord, and in the treasuries of [his own] house. At that time, Hezekiah cut off the gold from the doors of the temple of the Lord, and from the doorposts which Hezekiah had overlaid, and gave it to the king of Assyria."
>
> (II Kings 18: 13-18)

What need is there in paying tribute? For the Lord Yahweh's insured protection bears enough tranquility in eliminating the need to bend-over backwards (i.e., paying "all the silver" of Jerusalem and much of their gold, including the dismantling of the Lord's golden temple doorpost) in fulfilling the gratitude of a tyrant.

Either way, historically speaking, Jerusalem is spared.

However, One can speculate the true "sparing" of Jerusalem lay within their extortion and appeasement rather than divine intervention.

Jerusalem only survives more than a century before its fall to Babylonians. It is during the reign of David and Solomon that the original Hebrew language began to take form. As the short period of prosperity began (post Hittite Empire) the people of Israel establish a national language of proto-Hebrew script in accommodation from the profound script of their Aramaic neighbors;

the Phoenicians. An act resembling the Sargonic Akkadians adopting the Sumerian cuneiform script and creating their own Akkadian language.

Hebrew is to Phoenician as Akkadian is to Sumerian.

Once the Israelites established a secular language, they develop an independent nationality. A tribal, however so acclaimed, kingdom of Hebrew people united under the worship of the single god Yahweh. These different tribes are then held to a "universal Hebrew standard" known as the *Ten Commandments* or the "Hebrew Code of Law." In terms of historical influence, there exists little evidence in originality of the "Hebrew" people's overall contribution to war, diplomacy, mathematics, astronomy, or literature. Only adding onto existing content; for conquest, appeasement, and assimilation introduces the adoption of pre-existing ideals from previously existing, or contemporary, cultures such as the Sumerians, Egyptians, Babylonians, Hittites, and Assyrians. Having a multitude of corresponding, yet somewhat differentiating, attitudes in articulating a basic rationale of Our human condition. All being passed down from generation to generation of whichever empire reign supreme at any given time: entrusting their god to heed the spiritual pantheon, evidenced by historical testimony.

Under Hezekiah's sovereignty, the Assyrian king Sennacherib extorts tribute from Jerusalem to preserve their sovereignty. This event is further emphasized and explained not only by the Assyrians in their famous *Sennacherib's Prism,* but also by the Israelites in their second biblical book of Kings (18:13), depicting the invasion of Judah by the Assyrians. The Assyrian-form of imperial order reframes its form from the primitive attempt of central power by the Gutians (and later Hittites) to a new sustainable version of true authoritative consolidation.

All while the Assyrians take charge, the remnants of the Babylonian Empire absorb into the Semitic Chaldeans – including the regions of Sumeria/Babylonia. Remember, this constant conquest, appeasement, conquest, appeasement is cycling about throughout a core region in the Fertile Crescent. This Neo-Babylonian group of Chaldeans remain subject to the Assyrians yet begin to slowly recover (much like the Sumerians of the Ur III dynasty). By the end of the seventh century BCE, the Neo-Babylonian

Empire became re-established under the leadership of Nebuchadnezzar, destroyer of nations, at the fall of Nineveh and the Assyrians in c. 612 BCE. The re-institution of Babylonian rule dismisses the notion of religious tolerance. Including the religion of the Hebrew people at Jerusalem which, by c. 586 BCE, the Babylonians destroy (namely Solomon's Temple). For it is in Psalms 137:1 that laments, "By the rivers of Babylon, there we sat down, yea, we wept, when we remembered Zion..." A toll of great defeat, as the Hebrews of Judah are imprisoned by the tens of thousands under the word of Nebuchadnezzar while others are forced into a great disperse, initiating a period know to the Jewish history as the *Exile*.

That is until c. 539 BCE when the great Cyrus of Persia succeeds in conquest over the Neo-Babylonians. Most importantly, Cyrus establishes the Achaemenid Empire who instead of destroying conquered cities, like Babylon, would preserve them as a part of their empire – a more doctored version of Sargonic/Hittite/Assyrian imperialism. In conquering the Neo-Babylonians, the Persians liberate over forty-thousand Judahites from captivity. Upon their release, Cyrus, "...the great king of Persia, shows favor to the chosen people" (Ezra) in allowing them a successful return to their homeland; only to assist them in the rebuilding of the Second Temple by c. 516 BCE. Though the Persians were tolerant in allowing the reconstruction of the Jewish holy city (i.e., the province of Judah), they would not allow the complete restoration of a Jewish monarchy. This lack of restoring a Jewish king (and therefore kingdom) forces the high priests of Judah to wield dominant authority in the former lands of milk and honey. Hoping that one day a Jewish king will come to reclaim the Hebrew monarchy and thus renew their kingdom. It is during the next century that the fortunes of the Hebrew people are revived by strong priestly leaders (similar to ancient Sumerian *ensi*), including Nehemiah and Ezra who begin to preach of a Jewish king to come.

The multiculturalistic reign of the Persians allow yet another great diffusion of cultures and the mass sharing of ideas. The Persians generally accept religious tolerance as long as one paid their taxes and swore their allegiance to the empire. Remember, it is within a single generation from which the Temple is both destroyed and rebuilt – causing both events to be intimately intertwined by the age of a single family. Differentiating the ancient antagonists (namely Nebuchadnezzar) against the subsequent protagonist (Cyrus). For the generosity of Cyrus is held in high gratitude from the now-free Jewish people in comparison to the conquest-bent afflictions cast by the Assyrians and Babylonians. Evidence of such graciousness lay within the ancient Hebrew texts themselves; especially the second book of Isaiah which states,

> "It is I who says of Cyrus, 'He is My shepherd! And will [rebuild the Temple] along with Jerusalem...' Thus, says the Lord to Cyrus, His anointed king."
>
> (Isaiah 45)

Where the Hebrew word for "anointed king" translates to **messiah**, deeming Cyrus the Great as one of many messianic figures within Jewish literature.

Cyrus the Great's "grandson" Darius further conquers lands of people beyond the Levant, including the Ionian Greeks of the Asia Minor. These Ionian Greeks rebel the authority of the Persians, leading to the historic conflicts between the Greeks and the Persians (specifically under the reign of Darius's son Xerxes). The once independent city-states of Greece, much like the tribes of shasu, unite in dispelling Persian rule. In doing so, the imposition of the Persian Empire becomes obsolete to the Greeks. Though this is true, the inevitable result of the Greek victory brought forth internal conflicts amongst the Athenians and Spartans themselves. This civil dispute between two leading city-states would shake a mutual Greek diplomacy that results in the Peloponnesian Wars. This period of chaos allows the great Macedonian king Phillip II to conquer the many lands of dysfunction and appoint his son Alexander to initiate the Greco-Roman period by c. 332 BCE.

The early Greco-Roman period known as the "Hellenistic period" involves the most changes to the Hebrew culture (besides Persian influence). As Alexander took the helms of his father's empire, his conquest began leading him to the restored Hebrew people. For centuries, these people had remained under Persian rule, including the period of the Persians warring with the Greeks. However, like the Persians, Alexander offers the Hebrews to remain autonomous as long as they pay tribute and swear allegiance. By doing so, a sect of the Jewish people "welcome" the cultural assimilation enforced by the Hellenistic Greeks: from their religious philosophies to a burdening tax collection system (much as they did toward the Persians and their messiah Cyrus). After Alexander's death, the Jewish people found themselves amidst a raging power-struggle between Alexander's successors; each claiming rightful heir to the empire. As a result, the Hebrews are caught between the powers of the Seleucid state in the north and the Ptolemaic state of the south. Power amongst Judah shifting a number of times.

There is little existing evidence during this period that corresponds to the objective history of the Jewish people, in which discerning objective truth from subjective truth exists only with bias.

During the third century BCE, Ptolemaic rule in Egypt appoints the translation of the Hebrew scripture into Koine Greek (hence the term for "coining" a word or phrase). This translation, known as the *Septuagint*, is the basis for Eastern-Orthodox Christianity, yet is not accepted by traditional Hebrews nor Christians (due to its translation as holding much Greek influence).

Then, in year c. 168 BCE, the Seleucid king Antiochus IV outlaws the religious rights and traditions of the Jewish people outright – ordering the worship of Zeus as supreme god. Though Yahweh remain in the hearts of the Hebrew people, their faith is to be tested as they refuse to worship the false idol. The result of this Jewish anathema cause the Seleucid king to send his troops into Jerusalem, accounting for the mass slaughter of non-Hellenistic worshippers and the defiling of the Temple. These acts combine as the known "abomination of desolation" where traditional believers of Yahweh (who later establish themselves as the reknown Pharisees) are forced to flee the city. Those who remain in the city assimilate to the idolatry of Hellenistic influence – establishing the opposing sect of Sadducees (who revered the *Septuagint*). The overall response to this abomination emerge to what is now known as the Maccabean Revolt (c. 166 BCE). During this rebellion (led by a Judas Maccabeus of the Pharisees), the traditionalist Hebrews who were forced to flee Judah began retaliating against the impurities offered by Hellenistic influence of the authoritative Sadducees. In an all-out attempt to cleanse their holy land of impurity, the Pharisees sought to direct their frustrations towards the Hellenized Sadducees in a Jewish civil war. Antiochus IV, hoping to end the rebellion, supports the Sadducees during these battles. Only for the Maccabean Revolt to be the result of guerrilla warfare between the deposed Hebrews and their opposers. After "succeeding" in the rebellion, the Hebrew state claim independence once again but only for a brief moment in history. This short period of antiquity establishes the Hasmonean dynasty of Pharisees, whose events lead to the purifying of the Second Temple in c. 164 BCE. The festival of *Hanukkah* came to fruition in commemoration for the success of the Maccabean Revolt.

This subtle period of independence is thwarted by the Romans in their ascension to power soon thereafter. While at peace with the Romans, the Hasmonean dynasty began to experience yet another civil war – only this time amongst themselves for power. As an outsider looking in, a factioned Roman Empire capitalizes on an opportunity to seize Jerusalem and thusly Judah. Antigonus II, the last king of the Hasmonean dynasty, is defeated by the Roman-appointed king Herod the Great in c. 43 BCE. King Herod is prominently known for both his monumental building projects in Judah (including an expansion on the Second Temple) along with single handedly forging a brand-new aristocracy in the Hebrew kingdom. With this being said, the lasting impression of Herod's legacy is subjectively tainted as a tyrannical one. Heavy outbreaks of violence and rebellion soon follow the death of his kingship in the releasing of built-up grievances. The momentum of these uprisings ultimately lead to the Great Jewish Revolt of 70 CE; the first of three major Jewish rebellions against their Roman oppressors that would result in the destruction of the Second Temple. A consequence felt alongside the first near complete genocide of the Jewish people. The *Diaspora:* where both the Pharisee and Sadducee converge in their mass dispersion as wanderers once again.

Religion

Judaism is the foundation from which Christianity and Islam rest upon.

The testimony of the Hebrew Bible, known as the Tanakh, is considered to be generally canon with its competing religions. "Tanakh" represents the acronym "TNK," which relates each letter to its corresponding subdivision of the total work. Where:

- T = Torah (the Law) - consists of the Pentateuch (Genesis, Exodus, Leviticus, Numbers, Deuteronomy)

- N = Nevi'im (the Prophets) - consists of the eight prophetic books (Joshua, Judges, Samuel, Kings, Isaiah, Jeremiah, Ezekiel, the Twelve (minor prophets))

- K = Ketuvim (the Writings) - consists of the eleven books of wisdom-literature; separated by three categories: the Poetic Books (Psalms, Proverbs, Job), the Five Scrolls (Song of Songs, Ruth, Lamentations, Ecclesiastes, Esther), and the Historical Books (Daniel, Ezra, Nehemiah, Chronicles)

There exists no original TNK book; only copies of stories that are accumulated and further pieced together over *time*. For many of the books of the Tanakh are inserted later on a basis of redaction. Much like epics of Homer (which the ancient Greeks treat as their own biblical testimony), the status of the TNK in its entirety depends on a stretched period of oral restitution; followed by its further literary transmission. It is within only the subjective accommodation of a culture's upbringing that cause for differences amongst contemporary religions. Where, like the resembling cosmogenic creation of the Egyptians in Heliopolis with the Sumerians of Eridu, the Abrahamic account of creation calls for everything to come from the emergence of light out of a primeval watery abyss. The idea of a specified

"Seven Day Creation" derives from the recurring "number seven-based" theme of mathematical importance and almighty deities, bearing astrological implications associated with the seven visible heavenly bodies in Mercury, Venus, Earth, Mars, Jupiter, Our sun, and Our moon. Even the "Babylonian Bible" is named the *7 Tablets of Creation*. From the "seven fate-decreeing" gods of Egypt and Sumer with the "seven antediluvian *Apkallu*" rulers of pre-flood Mesopotamia, the number seven will forever hold important astrological-based ancestry.

Although the "Seven Day Creation" story and its following fables hold truth to all the followers of Yahweh, there comes a point in time where a division in agreeing on proper worship came to be. During the division of Solomon's kingdom (c. 930 BCE), the Israelites of the north began to adopt influence from its regional occupants: one of them being the Ugaritic people of northern Canaan (known today as Ras Shamra). Ugarit was a thriving trade hub compared to the likes of Byblos and Tyre during its time. The region is very diverse in cultural diffusion to such an extent that eight different languages of varying texts (which span in thousands) have been unearthed in the city today.

By c. 1400 BCE this minor civilization develops one of the oldest complete alphabets with substantial resembling order of modern alphabets (containing thirty different letters with corresponding dialectics). Though most presumably influenced by its great literate neighbors (Phoenicians, Egyptians, Mesopotamians), the Ugaritic people came under the rule of the conquering Hittites (and Egyptians) with their multicultural influence at the height of their innovative development. There is no dichotomy between the language and script of the Phoenicians, Ugaritic, and Hebrew people as they are all very similar in the sense that they are all considered *abjad*. These *abjad* languages resemble one another in that they are originally written entirely without vowels: where words carry only consonants and thus retain several possible meanings depending on the context. Thousands of Ugaritic texts (much like those of Sumer) unveil synonymous parallelism between their ancient literature and the works of later Hebrew testimony. There exists an irrefutable resemblance amongst supposed "original" scripts (in terms of structure, grammar, syntax, semantics, and other literary elements) and previously existing scripts. With the help of a proficient writing system, the people of Ugarit establish an Egyptian/Babylonian-type religion on the basis of mild monotheism – much like the Hebrew people will under a United Kingdom of tribes.

To understand the rich cultural history of the Abrahamic religions, One must first revisit the knowledge of its predecessors. The biblical scripture makes mention of the indigenous Canaanites and their morally corrupt religious ideals. The basis of Canaanite religion revolves around the supreme god "El" who is considered the "King of kings." The Ugaritic religion takes this narrative and expand on it – much like the Babylonians did with existing Sumerian tales.

The Ugaritic religion is based on an alteration of pre-existing cultural works from the Egyptians and Sumerians, however more directly from the Babylonians, in which a divine council commissions a **single** member of the assembly to carry out a divine decree. Though this form of proto-*monotheism* grants rule under a single helm, there remains still the existence of other gods. Overall, these gods and goddesses embody the cosmic order of the Universe and are responsible for the occurrence of natural events.

Only to be under the supreme guidance of a **single** member, head of the pantheon. In the case of the people of Ugarit, their leading god is titled "Ba'al," which simply translates as "Lord" – an allocation for the historical acknowledgement of such a divine title. No different than any other civilization, these gods carry the very qualities found within Oneself. As in the gods of the Ugaritic pantheon become established in the cultural image of its people. The entirety of their religion is foretold in many of their ancient texts, most notably the epic tales of the *Ba'al Cycle* (c. 1500 – 1200 BCE), which serves as a varying Semitic version of the already-known Babylonian tale of creation. As a result of the already-recurring "conquest and appeasement" the Babylonians had conquered Sumer with the intent of justifying their patron god (Marduk) in his rise to the head of a Sumerian pantheon. A necessity in justifying the "logic" and "reasoning" behind their patron god's miraculous rise to power: a common theme for conquest. This necessity is granted by the Babylonians in their account of creation in the "Babylonian Bible," known as the *Enuma Elish* (also referred to as the *7 Tablets of Creation*), resting as merely another varying version of the already-existing Sumerian tales of creation.

> "When on high the heaven had not been named, firm ground below had not been called by name, [there existed only] primordial Apsu, their begetter [existing as one with] Mummu [the 'main body'], and Tiamat, she who bore the gods, their waters commingling as a single body... Anu was their heir, rival of his father [Apsu]. Anu sired his image as Enki. This Enki was the master of his father, of broad *wisdom*, understanding, might in strength, and mightier by far than his [predecessors]."
>
> (7 Tablets of Creation)

The Babylonians honor the original Sumerian script by acknowledging the pantheon's cultural novelty. With the creation of gods by Tiamat from the primordial waters of Apsu; only the waters of Apsu now take deified form as the "father of Anu" (evidential transition between Sumerian and Babylonian work). Much like the Egyptian god Ra, the totality of this "father-god" manifests itself in **three creator forms**: one who creates reality; one who "creates" or establishes order; and one who creates *Life*. From these forms, the division of "pure *omnipotence*" is accounted for until the emergence of divine adversity – taking form as a godly descendant. Thusly consistent in the patriarchal recount of an heir claiming his father's throne.

> "They [the gods] disturbed Tiamat as they rushed here and there.
> Indeed, they distraught and tormented Tiamat, by their boisterous mirth in the dwelling of heaven.
> Apsu could not ignore their clamor and Tiamat was dumbfounded at their ways.

Their doings were loathsome to [their creators]. Offensive
and overbearing were their ways. Then Apsu, begetter of
great gods, cried out...
'Their ways are truly abominable unto me. By day I find
no relief, nor repose by night! I will destroy, I will wreck
their ways. That **quite** may be restored. Let us have rest!'...
'Destroy, my father, their rebellious ways. Then you shall
have relief by day and rest by night!'"

(Enuma Elish)

Hence the "novelty" of Sumerian folklore. Where instead of Enlil inflicting the apocalypse upon Mankind for his "noisiness" and His overbearing population increase, the father-god Apsu becomes similarly irritated at the "clamor" of his "children" in heaven. In deifying Apsu with an emphasis of the lesser gods as being "his children" reconfirms the underlying theme in the Sumerian creation story and the later Abrahamic account of creation. The theme of "god's children" being granted god-like powers; only for them to be ill prepared in the handling of said powers. Where, eventually, the supreme god lashes out at "his children" with vindication and remorse.

"When Apsu heard of this, his face grew luminous, because
of the **evil** he **planned** against his godly sons.
[The gods hear word of this plot and] lapsed into silence
and remain speechless. Superior in *wisdom*, Enki, the all-
wise, saw through the design...
As he poured sleep upon [Apsu] he loosened his crown;
removed his halo and put it on himself.
Having constrained Apsu, he slew him."

(Enuma Elish)

Cue to the corruption of patriarchy, as evidenced by its long-running historical manifestations. From Enlil over Anu, Osiris over Set, Zeus over Cronos, Caine over Abel, Jacob over Esau, Absalom over David, etc., the idea of a son/relative taking power from his blood predecessor originates from the roots of patriarchy. However, due to the immortality of gods, ancient theologians become forced to "drama-fy" this action of "passing the throne" by means of *deceit* (a capable quality within the image of Man, as the gods were created in Man's intuitive image). Once Enki establishes himself as head of throne, he conquers his enemies and rivals to inevitably instill heavenly peace;

> "In profound peace [Enki] rested in his sacred chamber,
> He named it Apsu... [It is in this chamber of Apsu where]
> the heart of holy was Marduk created.
> He who begot him was Enki, his father."
>
> (Enuma Elish)

Once the throne has been taken by Enki, Tiamat calls to exact vengeance for the "death" of Apsu by creating a monster of beasts known as the "Annunaki." These beasts are far too much for Enki to handle, so the pantheon agree in choosing his son and god of war, Marduk, to conquer Tiamat (which he does). Not only is Marduk successful in slaying Tiamat but in fulfilling the role as the "god of the gods." The king of kings; leaving the Babylonians successful in their quest to legitimize Marduk's kingship.

The Ugaritic people took this narrative and expand on it in order to similarly legitimize their own religious ideals. Comparable to the transition of Enlil's role, Enki, the wise **serpent** god, originally gives birth to Marduk in both Sumerian and Babylonian literature (the context for which may vary). As the previous head of the pantheon is surpassed by the chosen patron god – where the Babylonians retain Enlil's "fathership" but replace his kingship with Marduk; the Ugaritic people retain El's "fathership" but replace his kingship with their patron god "Ba'al." Carried over into the Ugaritic *Baal Cycle*, the names of prior Sumerian-based deities hold omittance with obvious title alterations. With this being said, the Ugaritic text opens up with,

> "Now, mighty Baal, son of Dagon..."
>
> (*Baal Cycle*)

The text, at any point, seems to fail in defining important characters such as this "Dagon" who is referred to as the father of Ba'al. Notice the name "Dagon" whose etymology is Hebrew in the word *dag* meaning "fish" and Ugaritic in the term *dgn* meaning "grain." Qualities both held by Enki, who gave Man both its agrarian lifestyle and the seven antediluvian "fish kings" known as the *Apkallu*. In understanding the Ugaritic adaptation of the *Enuma Elish,* One finds the clear candidate in identifying this "Dagon" with Enki, who creates the seven *Apkallu* and is thusly personified as one. This conclusion is drawn from the assertion of Marduk's role being replaced by the Ugaritic "Lord."

Where Marduk is the son of Enki, Baal is the son of Dagon.

The primary distinction between these two tales lies within the direct influence of the Egyptian creation story. The Egyptians had maintained control over northern Canaan until the Battle of Kadesh. So forth that direct Egyptian influence lingers amidst the ancient documents of the Ugaritic people. Where the primordial waters of "Apsu" and "Nu" are interchangeable, so are the qualities of Osiris and Set within Baal himself.

Remember the time of Hyksos rule as well, when the Semitic praise for the Egyptian god Set began its due diligence. The best qualities of Set and Osiris are then taken from the context of their creation story and placed within the chronology of Ugaritic religion. As Baal (like Set) is undermined in the choosing of kingship until he "rightfully" claims his role as protector of the gods. With such a claim calls for a duel amongst Ba'al and "death" (personified as the god Mot). This literary duel symbolizes the mortal battle between Life and death, since Ba'al is often referred to as the God of fertility (i.e., Life). Inevitably so, Ba'al is killed by Mot, only to have his sister/consort (named Anat) resurrect him in an inevitable reclaiming of the throne. In doing so, Anat destroys Mot by spreading the ashes of his burnt corpse all over the earth (alluding to Set's vindictive act towards Osiris). Though many details parallel the story of Set and Osiris with strong Sumerian influence, the story conforms to the multicultural appeal of the Canaanite continuum.

The evidence of Ba'al's influence lie directly within biblical testimony. For many "judges," including Gideon, held the title of *Lord* (known as *Jerubaal*). Also, many of Saul's sons withheld the title in name such as *Eshbaal* and *Meribbaal*. The intensive purpose in attributing the name "*baal*" for any tribal king is for a claiming of "lordship"; just as Ba'al literally means "lord" so does the godly name Yahweh (in which Yahweh is commonly referred to as "*Lord*"). Allowing Ba'al and Yahweh to be deviations of a single manifestation.

Another direct example of multicultural influence lie within the ancient Ugaritic *Baal Cycle*. Certain literary components seem to correspond nearly exactly with that of poems from the Hebrew Psalms, reading,

> "Let me praise you, Prince Baal [Lord]
> Let me repeat, Rider on the Clouds:
> Now, your enemy, Baal [Lord],
> Now you will kill your enemy.
> Now you will annihilate your foe.
> You will take your eternal kingship,
> Your dominion forever and ever."
>
> (*Baal Cycle*)

Now Psalms 92 and 145:

> It is good to give thanks to the Lord,
> And to praise your name, O Most High [Rider on the Clouds?] ...
> For, behold, your enemies, O Lord,
> For, behold, your enemies will perish...
> Your kingdom is an everlasting kingdom,
> And your dominion endures throughout all generations."
>
> (*Psalms 92 and 145*)

This is merely *one* example.

The overwhelming amount of evidence in comparing multiple religions stems from the overriding details that have carried from culture to culture in the regional continuum of Canaan. Indigenous Canaanites became the renowned Hyksos, who are later labeled as the wandering *shasu*, only to establish a monotheistic kingdom under the single divine lordship of Yahweh. Once the tribal Hebrew Kingdom split by c. 930 BCE, the neighboring influence of Ugaritic culture (which is a culmination of Sumerian/Egyptian/Babylonian influence) begin to permeate the newfound Semitic culture of the now northern Hebrews (even though there already exists the tainted-influence by the "religious idolatry" of their hypergamy Hittites – who had later adopted the Babylonian-based worship of Marduk). Not to mention the exclusive acts of Solomon in favor of Judah over these already-unsure Hebrews of the north. As the northern tribe of Israel begins adopting the diffused culture of the Ugaritic people and their neighbors, the inhabitants of southern Judah steadily hold a more traditional form of worship in "true *monotheism*" towards Yahweh. Where the differences in worship are merely separated by misinterpreted intricacies, such as the Lord's official name between *Yahweh* (*Jehovah*) or *Elohim*. The consequences of two differentiating Hebrew factions cause for multiple interpretations of divine decree between the Yawhist of the south (Judah) and the Elohist of the north (Israel).

The differences between these two factions are as obvious as they are blatant. So blatant, in fact, that their differences expose the logical fallacies of biblical testaments. Where the Bible's Old Testament accounts for *two* distinct creation stories (Genesis 1–2:4; Genesis 2:5–25), *two* distinct "fall of Man" tales (Adam and Eve; Enoch and the Nephilim), as well as *two* distinct flood stories (Genesis 6:5–8:22; Genesis 6:9–8:19). Also, do not forget the *two* separate calls of entering and exiting Egypt (first with Abram and Sarai; then with Joseph and later Moses), the *two* moments of Abraham's deception (first to the Pharaoh and second to Abimelech), and also the *two* different calls to Moses in receiving the *Ten Commandments* (first spoken to him, and then later *given* to him). The contradictions of biblical inconsistencies are more-times-than-not merely glazed over with unreasonable justification.

However, if One simply would read the scripture themselves, they surely will find the inconsistencies.

For example: Genesis 1–2:4 accounts for the commonly known "Seven Days of Creations." This account alludes to the *physical* creation of existence;

> "(1) In the beginning God created the heavens and the earth. The earth was formless, and void and darkness was over the surface of the deep, and the spirit of God was moving over the surface of the [primordial] waters. Then God said, 'Let there be light'; and there was light... (11) Then God said 'Let the earth sprout vegetation...' Then the earth brought forth vegetation."
>
> (Genesis 1:1–3 and 1:11–13).

This depiction of a "Seven Day Creation" is considered the *first* account of creation in Genesis:

Day 1: Creation of light

Day 2: Creation of the physical Universe

Day 3: Creation of the heavens and the earth

Day 4: Creation and separation of *day* and *night*

Day 5: Creation of all living creatures

Day 6: Creation of Man

Although this first creation story holds some Sumerian/Egyptian/Babylonian attributes, the second creation story of Genesis bears far more obvious details of pre-existing ideals. The verses of Genesis 2:5–25 begin to tell of a *second* account of creation after the Sabbath – one recognizably different than the first.

> "Now no shrub of the field was yet in the earth, and no plant of the field had yet sprouted for the Lord God had not sent rain upon the earth, and there was no man to cultivate the ground. Then the Lord God formed man of dust from the breath of life; and man became a living being."

(Genesis 2:5–7)

How could there be "no shrub of the field yet in the earth" and "no plant of the field yet sprouted" if on the third-day of Genesis chapter 1 god already establishes vegetation? Also, if on the sixth day god first creates Man in his image, then why the later account in the second chapter of Genesis claiming, "*Then* the Lord God formed man of dust from the breath of life; and man became a living being"? As in Genesis 1:25-27 claims Man being created *after* animals; only for Genesis 2:18-19 claiming Man as being created *before* animals (egocentric-based ideal). Or even Genesis 1:11-13 which claims plants as being created *before* Man; only for Genesis 2:2-7 to tell of plants being created *after* Man.

Hence the obvious "double account" foretold by opposing ideologies for the very same ideology. For this is merely *one* example.

The Yahwist script is the first Hebrew script to exist. The unified tribes of shasu under David and Solomon establish an exclusive language to their people, which leads to the ability of documenting their oral traditions. Scribes of the royal Temple began to document and collect the historical traditions that will make up the divine decree of the Hebrew religion. These specific stories are collected not with the purpose of an original congruence but for a more defined articulation in acknowledging the <u>human condition.</u> The beauty in ancient Hebrew testimony lies within its profound articulation of ethical reasoning and not within its originality. *Time* allows for these ancient intuitors to better express Our innate qualities by the already-existing accounts of their ancestors. Such as the genealogies of Genesis, which at face-value would seem to describe a literal genealogical branch of descendants. However, in context with its scripture, the genealogies of important figures, such as Noah, portray the patriarchies of the known world.

Where Noah's three sons represent not actual people of existing integrity but as symbolic distinctions of regional civilizations during those times. The Three Kings; avatars of artificial race – representatives of regional Man.

- Shem's Five Sons: Asia

  1. Elam – Persians

  2. Asshur – Assyrians

  3. Arphaxad – Babylonians (Chaldea)

  4. Lud – Lydians (Asia Minor)

  5. Aram – Syrians (Ugarit)

- Japheth's Seven Sons: Europe

  1. Gomer – Celtic, Cimmerians

  2. Magog – Scythians

  3. Madai – Medes, Kurds

  4. Javan – Ionian Greeks

  5. Tubel – Turks

  6. Meshech – Slavs of the Russian Plain

  7. Tiras – Estruscans

- Ham's Four Sons: Africa

  1. Mizraim – Egyptians

  2. Phut – Lybians

  3. Cush – Sudan, Ethiopia

  4. Canaan – Phoenicians

From the patriarchal descendants of Arphaxad (Chaldea) exist Abram, the symbolic "double account" of Noah (who bears the "Chosen Descendants"). It is within the very genealogy of Abram's patriarchy that solidifies the legitimacy of the specific Hebrew people (and later followers of Islam in the Arabian people). In Judaism, the lineage begins with Abram's second son, Isaac, who succeeds in relinquishing his throne between both his twin sons of Esau (nation of Edom) and Jacob (nation of Israel); only for Israel to prevail and birth itself twelve tribes in the form of "twelve children," each whom represent their own distinct civilized regions within Canaan. In that Joseph (Judah) being the favored amongst the twelve only to be perceived harshly in the eyes of his fellow brethren (neighboring tribes).

Original intuitions of Judaism sought to further articulate that of which was previously unacknowledged. These Hebrew scholars were not worried about plagiaristic unoriginality as long as they evolve the content of already-existing ideas; in order to couple the legitimacy of their Jewish history.

The collection of specific stories allows ancient Hebrew scholars to express their story of redemption with the intention of glorifying David and Solomon's unified monarchy.

Until the monarchy split.

In which the Israelites of the north sought to improve the already-established teachings of the southern Judahites. These "northern" accounts of divine testimony are discernible from the original Yahwist teachings in that the later "Elohist" scripture holds elevated literature and language. Also, the big difference between the Hebrew god as "Yahweh" or "Elohim" stems from the god's earthly capabilities. Yahweh is first conceived as an anthropomorphic god, just as the early Sumerians and Egyptians portray their god(s)) with physical existence – as the earliest depictions of the story *Adam and Eve* account for Yahweh as physically walking with Adam throughout Eden; only for Adam to actually "hide" from the all-knowing Lord. Where Yahweh himself intercedes on behalf of his own will, such as Yahweh directly liberating the Hebrew people from Egypt instead of Moses.

This differs from the Elohist perspective, as their god Elohim is far too divine to associate with Mankind directly. To make up for this divine awesomeness, Elohim uses intermediaries such as *prophets* or *angels* to relay his holy word on the account that Man cannot Himself communicate with Elohim. For Elohistic writers claim their god to be too high and majestic in heaven to be seen or heard by Man directly (yet somehow achievable by mortal prophets/priests [i.e., descendants of Levi]). Thus, the constant shifts between the biblical god as directly speaking with Man or by relaying his words via an intermediary.

The Elohist of Israel simply sought to cleanse the Yahwistic way by altering or "adding onto" the already existing testimony in Judah. The best example for this exists in the original *Ten Commandments* known to the Yahwist as the "Ritual Decalogue" found in Exodus 34:10–26. As the *Ten Commandments* are first *spoken* to Moses and his people in the form of "thunder and lightning flashes" until the occurrence of the Ritual Decalogue (the only form of *law code* within Yahwistic teaching) when Moses is instructed to write down the *spoken* words of Yahweh.

The Elohist then takes this idea to elaborate on the story's complexity, which originally contains hardly any *law codes* outside of the Ritual Decalogue. The northern Israelites expand on this scripture by establishing a much more complex code of law known as the Covenant Code. This code contains very resembling content of other pre-existing codes, most notably the Code of Hammurabi.

(place corresponding Hammurabi codes with Hebrew codes; i.e., an eye for an eye)

As the Elohist began to influence the testimony of Yahweh, the biblical convolution of coherency begins to take its form. For the modern state of the Tanakh rests on a long period of both oral restitution and its further literary transmission – much like epics of Homer's *Illiad* and *Odyssey*. The result of such restitution and transmission over long periods cause for subjective accommodation. It is within these subjective accommodations that cause for biblical contradiction and inconsistencies – thus the opposing views between the "northern Hebrew" and the "southern Hebrew." These contradictions and inconsistencies are evidenced by the narrative re-telling of many events (i.e., "double accounts"). It is within the re-working of telling these tales that redaction allows for the "cleaning up" of historical blemishes. Blemishes from both sides; both the Elohist and the Yahwist.

The book of Job and its proverbial verdict (as previously mentioned in prior chapters) seems to have already existed on account of the Sumerians in their composition *A Man and His God* (known also as the *Righteous Sufferer;* composed several centuries before the establishment of the Hebrew people). In knowing this, One begins to finally understand the blatant contradiction of the book of Job's testimony in competence with the rest of the Old Testament. For example, Job 38: 4-7 recounts how the Israelite god creates the stars *before* the creation of earth. However, if One looks back to the original testimony of Genesis 1:17, the text exposes the Israelite God as creating the stars *after* the creation of earth.

Due to the contrasting ideals amongst opposing Israelites, the scripture of the Old Testament became riddled with blatant contradictions.

However, these contradictions exist on the basis of one group attempting to justify their own culture ideals. An act no different than that of the cultures before them. Where the Elohistic "forty years of wandering" may correlate to the forty years of reign under David and then Solomon – who retain the kingship in Judah under Yahweh. In the eyes of the Elohist, the reign of any Yahwistic ruler is deemed as "years of misguidance." Only for the Yahwist to centralize the theme of "child sacrifice" as being tensely morally corrupt, for the Elohist seemed to have practiced in such. In the Elohistic account, known as the *Akedah*, Abraham appears to actually sacrifice Isaac in the making of covenant between himself and Elohim – entrusting that his God could "even raise the dead." The result of Abraham fulfilling the sacrifice of his son is absolving of his recurring deceitful sin with King Abimelech at Beersheba. This is evidenced by such later accounts in the New Testament book of Hebrews;

> "Abraham offered up Isaac…reasoning that God could even raise the dead, and so in a manner of speaking he did receive Isaac back from death."
>
> (*Hebrews 11:19*)

The purpose of going through with Isaac's sacrifice resembles the same divine consequences to that of Jesus's sacrifice. In that Abraham is willing to sacrifice his only begotten son for the total absolving of Mankind's sin.

Hence, the differing Israelites of the north acknowledging Yahweh as "Elohim" whose title shift holds high importance. For the title of "Elohim" in acknowledging the **single** god (Yahweh/Lord) is attributed over 2,600 times in the Hebrew Bible (Tanakh). In the Hebrew script, the making of a singular noun into a plural noun is made by adding a symbol that represents the two letters *im*. The general name "El" (as stated) derives from the main god of the pre-existing Semitic Levantine people (Canaanites), whose common title began to represent a generic root for divine importance. Though an individual god named "El" exists to many regional cultures (such as Ugarit's "Father God"), the general acknowledging of any god as "El ___" became common. So common, in fact, that later Hebrew scribes exemplify the culmination of specific microcosmic gods, represented as <u>El</u>, as being unified under the macrocosmic whole in <u>El</u>oh<u>im</u>. The descriptive pluralism of the word "Elohim" itself holds symbolic representation by asserting the notion of a **single** god who embodies the accumulative nature of any/every other existing god.

Overall, the objective existence of previous gods wielding unbelievable qualities rely entirely on a dependence of natural calamities and the exaltedness of the supernatural. In which the godly quality of *omnipotence* is "divided" amongst a class of specified super naturalness.

Thus *polytheism*.

Where *monotheism* differs entirely lies within a godly quality of pure *omnipotence* and thus a secular *omnipresence*. This quality becoming exclusive proves any division of power to be obsolete. For a truly **single** god of the Israelites, Yahweh (or the accumulative Elohim), manifests itself not during occasional super naturalness but beholds omnipotence throughout any/all aspects in Life.

The true intention of Abrahamic *monotheism* is to redefine the "one-and-only Almighty's" exaltedness as being beyond the realms of Nature:

"...but the Lord was not in the earthquake [and] the Lord was not in the fire; [only in the] sound of a gentle [*voice*]. When Elijah heard of it, he wrapped his face..."

(*I Kings 19:11*)

Throughout all the biblical scriptures, the presence of Elohim transcends Nature. Found not in the natural elements (earth and fire) but in the form of elevated nothingness (unseen: symbolized by the common "covering of One's face" in the presence of Elohim). This form came to view by the lingering irrelevance of previous "Father Gods" (Apsu, Anu, Atum) whose presence seemed to transcend their very own creations (including their subordinate gods). Just as the Ugaritic Canaanites had deified the previously inanimate *Apsu* of Sumer into their own "Father God," the ancient Israelites further deify the presence of all gods as a one cumulative omnipresence in Eloh*im*. Unlike the gods of Nature, who resemble Human-like deities, the one Elohim is viewed as trans dimensional. In which "his" (based on the masculinity of the Hebrew suffix '*im*') omnipresence is accounted for on the basis of historical testimony. Where Elohim presents "himself" lies not within the nature of natural events but in **every** event that has ever occurred – qualifying the qualities of Elohim as being *timeless*. In that Elohim is as present and effective as *time* itself; both exemplifying their omnipresence in the fourth-dimensional world even though they're not physically present. Both transcending of the superficial nature of timely existence.

Chapter 1 prompts the idea in which Our cognition retains an ambient, yet ambiguous, dimension that transcends *time*. This very idea corresponds to the Elohist redefining of their god, however still in the image of Man; via the image of Our *timeless* qualities of conscientiousness. As in this Elohistic god is innately innocuous and "vindictive" only by perception; for "he" acts with moral jurisdiction in authenticating the new Israelite articulation of ethical reasoning. Exemplifying yet another moment of transcending arrogance to produce unintentional introspection. Another egocentric attempt in further separating Ourselves from the nature of mortal existence.

It is within introspection that allows for the acclaimed knowledge of previous unclaimed ignorance to emerge. In order to cleanse ignorance, One must find *wisdom* – in that *knowing* relieves *not knowing*; *wisdom* relieves ignorance. The core principle found in all Abrahamic religions is the idea of a "fear of the Lord." This fear alludes to the self-humbling notion of acknowledging One's own ignorance. The innate ignorance of all mortal Life; allowing knowledge to be as unlimited as *infinity* itself. For the feeling of fear in the omnipresence of a superior intellect admits self-inferiority. An instinctual humbling mechanism due to an emerging microcosmic self-awareness of a grand macrocosmic order. It is within the act of introspection that allows the humbling of an individual's subjective existence to manifest itself. Knowing this "fear of the Lord" is to be *wise* and therefore to absolve the individual of sin – the sin of egocentric ignorance.

The book of Proverbs (proverb meaning *mashal*; Hebrew word for allegory/parable) maintains this idea of *wisdom* overriding sin. Where *wisdom* is referred to as *Chokhmah*, the emanation of a deified concept. The book in its entirety constantly relays *wisdom* as being goddess-like; providing the reader only with an inference of *her* divine presence as merely being an extension of Elohim himself. This assertion is emphasized by the following scriptures:

> "*Wisdom* shouts... *She* lifts *her* voice in the [town] square; 'How long, O naïve ones, will you love being simple minded? Behold, *I* will pour out *my* spirit on [Mankind] and *I* will make *my* words known to [Man]... [However] *I* stretched out *my* hand and no one paid attention; And [Man] neglected *my* council... [So] *I* will *also* laugh at [Mankind's] calamity... Then [Man] will call on *me*, but *I* will not answer...because they hated *knowledge* and did not choose the ***fear of the Lord***... So [Man] shall eat of the fruit of their own ways and be satiated with their own devices. For the waywardness of the naïve will kill them, and the complacency of fools will destroy them. But those who

listen to *me* shall live securely and will be at ease from the dread of <u>evil</u>."

(*Proverbs 1:20–33*)

The goddess of *wisdom* "pouring out her spirit [godly powers]" onto Mankind eerily resembles the same symbolism as *Inanna and the Huluppu Tree* where the *wisdom* goddess Inanna bestows the divine powers of "Me" onto her Sumerian subordinates (specifically Uruk, biblical Erech). Only the Sumerians chose *not* to uphold their "fear of the Lord" and therefore "ate from the fruits of their own ways" in their "disregard for knowledge"; resulting in their demise on the basis of their "naïve waywardness." But those who listen to *Wisdom* and the knowledge she offers will surely "be at ease from the dread of evil (ignorance)."

For "fear of the Lord" upholds *Chokhmah*; just as the Egyptians' "fear of the Pharaoh" upholds *Ma'at*; just as the Sumerians' "submission to their gods" upholds the divine powers of *Me*.

It seems as though introspection acts as an innate tool for rationalizing the unknown in its *infinite* entirety. So forth that One must learn the distinct nature of *themselves* (acknowledging their own subjectivity) before qualifying in an attempt at rationalizing the nature of objectivity. Where complex self-awareness calls for an instinctual yearning to absolve ignorance. To absolve ignorance is to purify One's state of **contentment** – much like the absolving of sin (evil) is to purify One's holiness. The symbolic anointing of Oneself is sought by reaching a designated level of **contentment**; achieved only by a conscientious state of moral purity. This is considered the problem with contemporary cultures (namely the Canaanites) in their "lack of moral purity."

This universal theme of absolving *sin* to claim spiritual **contentment** is primary to all ancient religions. Within the *knowledge* of an introspective transition remain a **content** understanding for the <u>human condition</u>.

The claiming of a timeless god beyond Our earthly realm provides a lasting significance to a culture of otherwise insignificance. Where the ancient Israelites contribute little in originality they strongly make up for in their profound ability to further articulate and preserve qualities of ethical value. Qualities of what it truly means to be a Human Being: One stricken with the <u>human condition</u>. Though these ideals already exist throughout the ancient Middle East, the distinct chronological narrative in which they were told did not. As in the Abrahamic narrative retains a lot of spiritual and cultural heritage common to the ancient Middle East yet holds an isolated value. With that being said, the obvious commonalities are evidential within the biblical testimony themselves; depicting the Abrahamic faith against the backdrop of its regional occupants. Understanding the context in which these cultural comparisons derive stems from a basic understanding of the ancient lands themselves. And if an individual is ignorant to the historical testimony of the ancient lands themselves, they are in turn ignorant to the historical testimony of biblical scripture.

Which is not a terrible thing, however, a distinction factor that implies blind faith.

Thousands of years grant for a mastered redaction of ancient testimony. This mastered version of ancient scripture allows for the "originally intended purpose" of all ancient texts to come to light – that being a further understanding of Our own <u>human condition</u>. Allowing an articulate form of ethical reasoning to become comprehensive for the laymen. In which Judaism transforms the regional commonalities amongst Levantine cultures by further elaborating the theme of their ethical narratives. Where the primitive ignorance of prior intuitors did not allow for them to comprehensively articulate the meaning of their stories – even though the original theme of these stories were preserved by the intuition of primitive introspection. For how could One define "love" if they are ignorant to the word itself? The moral motif of the ancient Hebrew doctrine gives history this word for "love" (metaphorically speaking). Otherwise the moral teachings of ancient knowledge could only be "felt" and not "known"; felt by the innate unacknowledged ignorance of days past (viewed as morally corrupt). Only by acknowledging One's innate ignorance (and thus their "fear of god") will they begin to find **contentment** in this Life.

The ancient Israelites are able to justify and rationalize the vindictive nature of their god; an ability lost to those of neighboring cultures (primarily

Mesopotamia). For the natural calamities of Sumer were enough reason to acknowledge vindication, although seeming *random* and *unjustified*, namely for the sake of it. Instead, the god Elohim presents punishment for adjudication; for not having "fear of their Lord." Establishing a moral basis for proper existence. In which the Abrahamic ideals of vindication are exemplified through not only natural phenomena but by the now recognized "Human nature" of cyclical conquest and consolidation. Where the Elohim presents himself throughout all aspects of life (especially wrath-by-conquest to "teach a lesson to false worship"), the previous justification for natural calamity posed the only appearance for anthropomorphized deities.

With this, the ancient Hebrews are able to logically rationalize their historic tribulations of being conquered; as Elohim penalizing Mankind (namely his chosen Hebrew people) for their constant moral corruption (sin). When in reality, the tribal Hebrews were widely inferior to their surrounding neighbors and thusly more susceptible to being conquered. The constant moral corruption amongst the Jews equates to their appeasement towards ignorance (*evil*) and the depriving results of maintaining fearlessness toward its existence. Only in fearing the unlimitedness of Elohim (acknowledging the existence of One's own ignorance) can an individual thrive in prosperity. Labeling the tragic moments of biblical testimony as necessary evils to further combat evil. [*negative multiplied by a negative equals a positive...?*]

All of the Abrahamic religions derive from the basic discontent of the ancient Israelites with their culture milieu. In their entirety, the three religions of Abraham reside as cultural critiques of its preceding heritage. For the content contention between contemporary cultures cause for the culmination of calamities within the continuum of Canaan – in which Christianity and Islam are comprised.

IV. Christianity

History

What is truth?

Once Nebuchadnezzar imposes the sixth century BCE Jewish *Diaspora,* many reforms to Jewish culture take place in ultimately manifesting themselves into what is known as Early Christianity. To firmly comprehend these reforms, One must accept the objective of introspection which aims to omit subjective bias.

It was the great king of Parsa who liberates the captive Hebrews from the Neo-Babylonians, the now-grateful Hebrews pay homage to their liberator; deeming him Cyrus the *messiah.* He who brings restoration to the Temple and therefore the reclaimed earthly unity with Yahweh. Other than the soon-to-be messiah Jesus Christ, Cyrus is the *only* figure in the Hebrew scriptures who is legitimately referred to as "Yahweh's anointed one" i.e., the *designated* messiah, chosen by the Lord *Himself.*

The idea of awe-stricken adornment toward Cyrus *and his dynastic family* was not uncommon amongst the various peoples whom they liberated. In fact, the ancient Egyptians of the time had hailed Cyrus's son Cambyses as the actual Pharaoh of their land. Even the neo-*ensi* of Babylon claimed Cyrus synonymously with Marduk – the messianic liberator of the gods. This equation of patron gods and imperial liberators is evidenced perhaps best with the dynasty of Cyrus yet was not uncommon. For Alexander the Great saw such synonymity.

Relaying the notion of any high priests of those liberated (whether it be the Hebrew, Egyptian, Babylonian, etc.) believing whole heartedly in their liberators (namely the *Cyrus dynasty*) as being assisted by none-other than their own patron god(s). Thusly claiming their god(s) as "choosing" Cyrus to free their people. Where else would the generous benevolence of the Persian-people stem?

Thus, the birth of the Hebrew *messianic movement*; originating from post-Persian liberation. This messianic movement was met by the graciousness of Cyrus, giving hope to a generation who were otherwise hopeless. By the time the Second Temple is constructed, the messianic prophecies of the Old Testament began to take form. The first being from Isaiah, whose book is considered a collection of two or more oracles – distinct to separate periods in history. *Proto-Isaiah,* chapters 1-39, are considered the actual "words of the prophet" in foretelling the judgement of Israel by their god; *Post-Isaiah* (which could be considered two separate works), chapters 40-66, foretelling and acknowledging the presence of Cyrus and thus the newfound messianic prophecies. Namely Isaiah chapter 7 [which is later re-rendered into *Proto-Isaiah* in order to allude a foreshadowing of the coming messiah] when the prophet assures a Hebrew king from the kingdom of David to save Judah from its impending invaders. It is specifically from these words which give credence to the Gospel's book of Matthew 1:23 – where the doctrine of the virgin birth takes form.

> "And [Ahaz] said, hear ye now, O house of David; Is it a small thing for you to weary men, but will ye weary my God also? Therefore, the Lord himself shall give you a sign; Behold, an *almah* ['virgin'] shall conceive, and bear a son, and shall call his name *Immanuel.*"
>
> (Isaiah 7:13-14)

It is within the *implied* interpretation of the Hebrew word *almah* (meaning young marriageable woman) from which the ideal "virgin mother" gives divine birth, specifically to a child by the name "Immanuel" which in Hebrew translates as "God [being] with us." In that the prophet Isaiah promises King Ahaz of Judah a soon-to-be messiah (whom of which "God is with") to protect the Judahites from its soon-to-be oppressors: the Assyrians and later Neo-Babylonians. Only for this particular messiah to parallel the very agent who restores the earthly worship of Yahweh by the liberation of said oppressors. This *first* messiah became known as Cyrus the Great.

It is by the basis of the Persian religion from which their profound "kindness" originates. For it is true; where stems the motive for these conquerors' benevolence?

This must've been an ethical position posed to those ancient Hebrew scholars of the day. In such awe, they began to learn the principle nature of their liberator's ancient culture – that of the *messianic*-based Zoroastrianism. By c. 516 BCE, the spiritual acquiescence of a Davidic warrior-King-to-come, and thus the Hebrew *messianic movement,* began to take place.

As previously acknowledged, the early Greco-Roman period known as the "Hellenistic Age" brings forth the most changes to the ancient Hebrew culture (outside of the profound Persian influence). As Alexander the Great takes the helms of his father's empire, his conquest leads him to the restored Hebrew people. Similar to the Persians, Alexander grants the Hebrew people autonomy so forth they pay tribute and swear allegiance to his empire (though this "autonomy" stems from the authority of Egypt). By doing so, the higher-sect of Jewish power (known as the Sadducees) inevitably "welcome" the cultural assimilation of the Hellenistic Greeks, again, from their religious philosophies to a burdening tax collection system. In response to Hellenistic influence, traditional Jews (known as Pharisees) attempt to return their people to the traditional ways of antiquity. These Pharisees sought to direct their frustrations toward the Hellenized Sadducees in an all-out Jewish civil war. What became known as the Maccabean Revolt is merely the result of guerrilla warfare between the two sects of Hebrews. Warfare within one culture once again: the parting of blood-ties by starting apartheids.

"Succeeding" in the rebellion, the Pharisees claim independence but only for a brief moment in history (as celebrated by the tradition of *Hanukkah*). This short period of antiquity is established, and inevitably tarnished, by the acclaimed Hasmonean dynasty of Pharisees. The dynasty itself see's its first "downfall" shortly after the former-Pharisee named John Hyrcanus (who declares Jewish independence) accepts *both* governorship and the title of

High Priest (which opposes the principles of the Pharisee) in response to Seleucid oversight. It is John Hyrcanus who begins the growth of the Jewish vassal-state by means of "non-Pharisaic" acts; namely his *forced-conversion* campaign of expansion (a Hellenistic trait) against both the Samaritans and Idumeans (of Edom). This act of forced conversion contrasts the will of Elohim, as One cannot *force* the *fear of the Lord.* An act whose equal and opposite reaction will inevitably cause for the dynasty's collapse.

John then seeks out in establishing a sacrosanct-relationship with the growing Republic of Rome in light of the foreseen Seleucid downfall. The first intimate relationship between the Romans and the "chosen people." One which would seem to only protect those Hebrews in power, namely the Sadducees. It was by this downfall of John where Hillel the Elder articulates the dictum of "Not believing in thyself until the day of thy death." For John Hyrcanus had lost his Hasmonean ways.

After his death in c. 104 BCE, John's eldest son Judas Aristobulus I (*"Judas"* being the Hellenized form of the Hebrew name "Judah" and *"Aristobulus"* being the Greek epithet meaning "he who best advises") continues his father's downward legacy in wanting to acclaim both civil authority (governorship) and religious authority (high priesthood). In John Hyrcanus' will, however, he attempts to instill a "separation of priesthood and governorship" by giving governance to his wife and the power of high priesthood to Aristobulus. This urge of power causes Aristobulus to not only imprison three of his four brothers (all whom could challenge the "chosen" heir-apparent) but imprisons and starves his own mother to assure his role as both high priest and governor. An act of corruption that will cause Judas Aristobulus to deem himself "the Ethnarc King (basileaus) of Judaea." A title which is foretold to only belong to the soon-to-be-messiah of the lineage of David, for the Hasmoneans descend from the lineage of Levi. Not only a this, but is within the post-exilic concept that a Davidic warrior king should not be fulfilled until the *end of days.* An eschatological conundrum which is the guiding force behind many disputes of modern times – namely between the Palestinians and the State of Israel.

The out-of-nowhere death of Judas Aristobulus is thought to be the result of an undiagnosed ailment: though the Pharisees saw his death as retribution from Yahweh. Similar to his father, the passing of kingship went first to the widow and later to an heir apparent. Only the widow of Judas, named Salome Alexandra, frees and marries her once-imprisoned brother-in-law, Alexander Jannaeus, to replace the vacant throne.

Alexander Jannaeus (c. 103 – 76 BCE) is no different than that of his predecessors; a supposed Pharisee and tyrannical leader of constant oppression. Though a tyrannical leader, Jannaeus is thought to have officially established the Hasmonean Court of Judaea, the Great Sanhedrin. This assembly of Jewish leaders, composed primarily of Hellenized Sadducees, exemplifies an obvious Greco-Roman influence of newfound governance. One which shifts *heavenly* guidance to the hands of *earthly* power. One which inevitably differentiates the "omnipotence of Elohim" from the "omnipotence of Man," emphasized by the later Judeo-Christian phrase *"Render unto Caesar what is His!"* By the basis of Man's constant conquest and appeasement there exists a distinction of *earthly* power from *heavenly* guidance. For the authority of the Sanhedrin (supported by Rome) represents the *earthly* incarnation of Yahweh's *heavenly* omnipresence.

It is by the Sadducee-based idolatry of Alexander that justifies his crucifying of over eight hundred Pharisees in the year c. 87 BCE to end the civil warring. In the interest of his own house, Alexander and Queen Alexandra bear two sons in naming them Hyrcanus II and Aristobulus II. Both whose naming give further credence to a long-held tradition of Man's patriarchal society regardless of culture.

From the regnal names of Egypt to the Sumerian epithets of affiliation, the patriarchal passing of a father's name (known as a *patronymic* surname) unto his heir(s) assure the ancestral sanctity of a specific people/person – namely powerful Men of prominent influence. The Romans, who at this point posses heavy influence over the region, follow a complexly dignified form of patronymic labeling in their *Tria Nomina* or "Three Names" which is comprised of the following:

- Praenomen – "before name" or "personal name"

- Nomen – "family name" or "dynastic name"

- Cognomen – "nickname" or "by name"

Three names of patriarchal inclusion, similar to the three creator forms of many ancient gods. The *praenomen* is generally used by close friends and family while the *nomen* indicates the generational name (*gens*) or "dynastic family name." The *cognomen* is later implemented for distinguishing prominent members of any given gens, as it became common for the *praenomen* and *nomen* to both be passed down, for they are both forms of **filiation**. The *cognomen* itself, however, is given by the basis of virtue, distinguishing physical attributes, or in the case of adoption. This is best exemplified by the adoption of Gaius Octavius by Gaius Julius Caesar. In which Gaius Octavius retains his *praenomen* "Gaius," adopts the *nomen* "Julius Caesar," and adds an *adoptive cognomina* suffix (usually -*anus* or -*inus*) to the stem of his original surname: giving the adoptee's new name as Gaius Julius Caesar Octavianus.

Succeeding the name of prior patrons is not distinct to any one civilization. The passing on of patriarchal surnames authenticates the eternal spirit of One's family dynasty – a long held tradition granted by Our human condition. A *name* or *title* that subjectively separates each individual family on the basis of their genetic (or adoptive) ancestry. By naming and renaming, whether it be the title of *Sargon, Horus, Marduk, Baal, Cyrus, Alexander, Caesar,* etc., the preservation of essence in any ancestor's presence remains eternally present.

(*think on this*)

The Greek-based titles of "Hyercanus II" and "Aristobulus II" then expose the corruption of Helenized false-Pharisees. Though this is true, the two brothers develop opposing ideals in the wake of their father's death. Once of age, Hyrcanus II is appointed high priest *and* king to reorganize the Sanhedrin in following the way of the Pharisee. This action angered the

Sadducees who are then ordered to be removed and reassigned to their own towns outside of the holy city. Not going out without a fight, the Sadducees recruit the help of the new king's brother, Aristobulus II, who resembles the ideals of his father by supporting the Sadducee over the Pharisee. The two brothers meet near the city of Jericho where Hyrcanus II is forced to renounce his kingship and office of priesthood at the hand of Aristobulus the younger.

Remember the title *Hyrcanus* from the Hasmonean John Hyrcanus: he who had enforced the conversion of Idumeans to Judaism. The divine consequence for such potent proselytization is thought to have led to the inevitable birth of the Jewish Idumean known as Antipater (who held the patriarchal surname of his father, Antipater I). Consequently enough, it is the renamed *Hyrcanus II* who is later advised by this Antipater the Idumean to reclaim the throne from Aristobulus II. A reclaiming of the throne that will be hijacked by the palms of Pompey Magnus during Rome's conquest of Syria.

The Hasmonean dynasty itself is analogous to the sovereignty of the ancient Judges from the past. In that an acclaimed Jewish independence flourishes until an act of abomination forces the condemnation of Yahweh's holiness: beginning with the Arc of the Covenant by the Philistines, later with desecration of the Holy of Holies by Pompey's entrance. With this being said, Hyrcanus II, under the advisory of Antipater, concedes first to Pompey and later shifts to Julius Caesar. The latter comes at the granting of the Jewish people valor in the eyes of Caesar thanks to Antipater and his forces helping liberate the Roman dictator at the Siege of Alexandria in c. 47 BCE. This form of elevated prestige bestows upon Antipater the position of Judaea's first Roman procurator (imperial tax collector) and establishes Hyrcanus II as Jewish basileus/ethnarch (i.e. "King of the Jews"); a title which is granted to any ethnarch of Judaea. It is due to Antipater's position as procurator which allows him to promote within the interest of his own house, establishing the famed Herodian dynasty.

By this point in Mankind's history, as recently acknowledged, a significant paradigm shift occurs. One which relays the notion of the division between *earthly* omnipotence and *heavenly* omnipresence. This notion is emphasized by the rendering unto god what is his and unto Caesar what is His – alluding to the divine existence of any Roman emperor (i.e., *Caesar*) by way of Rome's imperial dominance.

Seven years after the assassination of Julius Caesar in c. 44 BCE, Herod, son of Antipater the Idumean, becomes the sole ruler of the Roman province Judaea. The maintenance of the Herodian dynasty in power stems from their ability to provide a proficient stream of collected taxes by their Jewish occupants. King Herod, an acclaimed "Jew" himself, sought to win over the support of his subordinates at the expense of heavy persecution towards those who opposed him – namely the Pharisees. The extent of his persecutions went as far as the condemning of his own two sons, named Alexander and Aristobulus IV, who were executed by blame of treason. Forty misguided years of rule under the sub-tyrannical leader. All in all, the dynastic title "Herod" itself connotes the times of Roman-Judea in division.

The death of Herod in c. 4 BCE causes the appointment of his son Herod Antipas to rule as ethnarch over the Roman-Jewish provinces for the next forty-three years. These forty-three years of reign directly parallel the forty-three years of Roman rule under Giaus Julius Caesar Octavianus Augustus – he who had directly appointed Herod Antipas as ethnarch in the first place. This forty-plus year reign of "misguidance" reveals itself in similar fashion to the "forty years of wandering" imposed by the ancient Elohist onto the ancient Yahwist. Acknowledging the northern Israelites in their perceiving the kingdom of David and Solomon as years of wandering in the allegorical *wilderness of ignorance*. Where the entirety of the dynasty of Caesar Augustus (known as the Julio-Claudian dynasty) act as a representative for the worldly powers that be; that being Rome. First with Octavius then following with Tiberius, Caligula, Claudius, and finally Nero. Seemingly enough, it is by the supposed word of the Julio-Claudia appointed ethnarch Herod Antipas from which John the Baptist is beheaded.

Consequentially enough, Antipas is usurped in power by his nephew/brother in law named Agrippa I – a title which aims to contrast Agrippa the Great against his dynastic family. Unlike Herod the Great and Herod Antipas before him, the three years of Agrippa's reign are considered "a period of relief for the Jewish people" at the time. Agrippa the Great, like most of his Herodian family members, is raised (and therefore educated) from an early age in the Roman Imperial Court. This opportunity is expedited by the Roman emperor Tiberius who likely imposes the name/title *Agrippa* against the otherwise *Herod*. For the name "Herod Agrippa I" was not Agrippa's name by birth but instead was Marcus Julius Agrippa. A name that derives from the emperor Tiberius' father-in-law *Marcus Vipsanius Agrippa*, the most trusted friend and general of Caesar Augustus himself.

The favored Herodian Agrippa is educated in congruence with the royal family of Rome alongside Tiberius' son Drassus and the young Claudius (who will eventually become emperor; the first emperor to be born outside of Italy). It is by this favor of Tiberius which allows Agrippa to challenge the throne of Herod Antipas and claim himself king of Judaea by the year c. 41 CE.

The kingship of Agrippa is met during the same year as the assassination of the Roman emperor Caligula; shifting the power of Rome towards Claudius (both whom were companions to Herod Agrippa himself as they grew up together in Rome). However, before Caligula's death, Agrippa is able to convince the emperor of his right to the throne. The persuasion of Agrippa causes Caligula to exile Herod Antipas from Judaea and into Gaul, perhaps a divine consequence for the beheading of John the Baptists by Antipas. Though only king for three years, Agrippa leaves a candid legacy in comparison to his Herodian predecessors.

Considered to be the last true king of the Herodian dynasty, Agrippa the Great passes on his legacy to his son Agrippa II. This new king is famed for his New Testament appearance as the king of Judaea, alongside his sister Berenice, during the trial of renowned Paul the Apostle. By this point in Judeo-Roman history, the Hebrew people are struck once again in the accumulation of built up grievances.

Let's not forget of the assistance of Antipater to Julius Caesar who then claims decrees of favor toward the Hebrew people. One such decree, known as the *religio licita*, legally protects the religious tenets of Judaism – under the profound assumption that the dynasty of Caesar exist with divinity. Hence, the rendering unto Caesar's *earthly* omnipotence. This assumption stems from the fact that Julius Caesar himself became the first known Roman emperor to become **deified**; elevating his *name* and dynastic existence in competence with any and all gods. A granting of an apotheosis no different than *Gilgamesh*, the Egyptian *Pharaoh*, *Cyrus*, or *Alexander* (to say the least). A macrocosmic act that reveals itself on the basis of the microcosmic patronymic *naming* and *renaming* of any successor from predecessor.

The deification of Julius Caesar came by approval of the Roman Senate on 1 January 42 BCE in thanks to his successor Augustus. This practice of divine exaltation introduces the spirit of the emperor as being worshiped in synchronicity with the Roman state itself. By giving praise to one's ruler, they in turn give subliminal praise to the state (or vice versa). For it is the ruler of Rome who control's the empire's continued prosperity. Whose prosperity is initiated by what is known as the *Pax Romana* period of Roman peace, brought forth by Julius Caesar and carried out by Caesar Augustus.

The biggest shift of arrogance from Julius Caesar to Caesar Augustus is within the application of the title of *divus* meaning "divine." It is Augustus who is renamed Gaius Julius Caesar *Divi Filius,* that is Augustus: son of the divine Julius Caesar. One who is *given* divinity by the Senate (Julius Caesar) and one who is divine by natural extension (Caesar Augustus). Similar to *Cyrus* and *Alexander* before them, the tradition of giving divine praise to any earthly/living leader is as unoriginal as the development of agriculture. This tradition of worship depends on the overall prosperity of the state, which, in turn, establishes what are known as *imperial cults*. These cults were used to worship those "gods" who directly influence the day-to-day lives of their subordinates. Of those worshipped, the state's military leader represents the *observed* protector (in contrast to the *unseen* protector(s) i.e., the pantheon of god(s)). Giving further credence to the distinction of Man's *earthly* omnipotence against god(s)' *heavenly* omnipresence. Though this is true, these events are seemingly not new, for remember the time of ancient Egypt's *cult of Amun* in contrast to the Pharaoh. Whose dichotomy is further rendered at the hands of Alexander the Great and his own imperialistic cult.

Julius Caesar is able to recognize the success of Alexander's imperial cult in relation to his successful conquests. Having been largely successful himself,

Caesar represents a thriving Roman state on the basis of his guidance (*genius*). Unlike Alexander, however, Julius Caesar is the first ruler of the *Roman Republic* to resemble an absolute "king" – as "kings" were despised and Rome itself was founded on their deposition. It is by this resemblance which calls for Caesar's assassination and the desecration of his legacy. Only for his successor, Augustus, to learn from the mistakes of his predecessor and inevitably revamps the image of Caesar while fulfilling his goal of dynastic deification.

Augustus understood the necessity of distinguishing himself against Caesar in order to gain back the trust of the Roman senate and the Roman people. By doing so, he would follow the act of linking himself to the Roman state (in prosperity) by the pursuit of adopting an imperial cult. This imperial cult would be the intermediary in maintaining the people's trust by alluding to an Augustus who did not seek to become a monarchal king. By his actions, such as his returning of the Senates' "full power" and his surrendering of provisional power, the emperor is able to anoint himself as a *just* ruler (though not a "king"). An allusion blatantly ignored by his predecessor. For Augustus would allow the state's status to speak for itself.

The illusion of Augustus' success in the implementation of apotheosis in comparison to his adoptive father stems from his incorporation of traditional Roman practices within the establishing of his imperial cult. In order for the people of Rome to appease to the idea of king-like worship, the imperial cult of Augustus had to disguise itself in the appearance of an independent Roman institution. One which glorified the emperor seemingly without the emperor's input. For example, after his success in deposing Marc Antony, the imperial cult of Caesar Augustus vote for any banquet of any kind to include the libation of the emperor's *genius*. A libation is merely the ritual of pouring out wine or olive oil in commemoration while *genius* reflects the subjective consciousness (soul) of each individual – in this case the individual being Caesar Augustus.

The worship of the Caesarean *genius* act as an unofficial form of worship, for the worship of an individual's *genius* does not imply their divinity. As a result, the act of libation in the name of Augustus reaffirms his holistic omnipresence without an implied omnipotence. Subliminal praise which is further revealed by the imperial cult of Augustus to align their emperor with patron deities such as Hercules and Romulus. In comparing Augustus to other prominent gods, the subsequent praise of said gods is shadowed by the emperor's *genius* outright. This subsequent praise is best emphasized by the cult's imposition of the emperor's personal name to be included alongside the names of the Roman pantheon in both private and public hymns.

Augustus continually demonstrates his actions as being for the benefit of the state of Rome and not for himself. The emperor would claim any honors the people awarded him only in parallel to the success of Rome. Again, after Augustus had defeated Marc Antony, the emperor calls for the construction of what is known as the *Forum of Augustus,* a public square of social interaction. Within the forum is built a temple dedicated to Mars, god of war, the Roman redaction of the Babylonian Marduk. In constructing this symbol of dedication, Augustus is able to further align himself with the god Mars as being "from the house of Mars." No different than that of Alexander the Great in his success at his claim to being from the house of Zeus.

The people of Rome took comfort in the benevolent actions of Augustus to ensure the state's revival. Unlike the former Julius Caesar, Augustus is able to play down his divine exaltation in aligning himself alongside the *people.* By refusing praise, He receives praise: a reciprocation of communication. This uniformity of the state and its people is squandered at the egocentric hands of Augustus successors. Successors who reflect the actions of a prior predecessor.

Once the imperial cult is established, it subsequently becomes corrupted. First by Tiberius, who sought to cleanse the entire empire of "non-Roman" cults (for example the cults of Isis, Mithras, etc.) including the foreign messianic Judaism. This cleansing of foreign cults further propagates at the hands of Caligula who radically shifts the meaning of Caesarian *genius* worship from the *divi filius* to Caligula himself. Caligula's drastic reforms went as far as replacing the heads of many godly statues, including female ones, in the enforcing of his divine worship as the embodiment of any and all gods.

The obvious attempts of Caligula to be seen as a sort of god-king lead to his inevitable assassination – a cause and effect no different than that who he was named after. The successor to Caligula is his paternal uncle, Claudius Caesar Augustus, who follows the narrative of his adoptive grandfather Augustus by the restoring of Roman virtues from its previous reign. Though thought to be an observant ruler, the selfless sovereignty of Claudius is met too by assassination. Wife/niece of Claudius and sister to Caligula, the young Agrippina is thought to have poisoned her husband in a coup attempt to place her son Nero in power (who was not the son of Claudius and therefore not an heir apparent). Nero the infamous, he who peaks the accumulated grievances of the Judeo-Roman people.

Agrippa the Great is considered to be the last true king of the Herodian dynasty due to Claudius' reformation of imperial governance. Thanks to Julius Caesar, the Hebrew people were able to claim an independent monarchy under the guidance of a Roman tax collector known as a *procurator,* the first being Antipater the Idumean. Where the *Jew* himself was a king (governor) in contrast to the Roman-appointed tax collector. This idea of an independent Jewish monarchy is soon diffused at the implementation of a Roman *prefect* or imperial governor. Due to this implementation, the reversal of roles between *tax collector* and *governor* shifts from the hands of the Judae-Roman people themselves to the hands of their oppressors. Where the *Jew* is now the tax collector in contrast to the Roman-appointed governor.

Whether the Judeao-Romans assumed an independent monarchy themselves, they were always under the macrocosmic guidance of Rome. Due to this, the idolatrous influences imposed by successive Roman prefects causes constant Hebrew rebellion – namely within the cities of Egypt's Alexandria and the coastal city of Caesarea in Judaea. Rebellions which were fought amongst the people themselves between those who accept idol worship (*Samaritans/ Syrians/Greeks)* and those who do not (antiquated *Jews).* The reoccurrence of civil strife between *those heretics* and *us, the practical.*

The overall legacy of these successive Roman prefects is best characterized by those Judeao-Roman people who refuse to accept any graven images of their gods – even the now *earthly* god known as the Roman emperor (i.e.,

Caesar). The prefects of Judaea were expected to conform to the Jewish *religio licita* in response to the people of Judaea's acceptance of Caesar's *earthly* dominion. This acceptance, however, does not usurp the power of Caesar over Yahweh. The acceptance merely couples the laws and observations of the *heavenly* Yahweh with that of the *earthly* Caesar. Knowing this, the insertion of any image of Caesar (albeit coinage, statues, busts, army standards, etc.) is considered blasphemy by idolatry to the Jewish people. Idolatry; the act of idol worship. An act which aligns itself within the principles of antiquated Greco-Roman society. Contrastingly, in the eyes of the antiquated Hebrew, the acceptance of Caesar as an *earthly* god blatantly contradicts their monotheistic tenants in Judaism's foundation.

It is by the extant of Roman ignorance/lack of appeasement in relation to Jewish law that cause for the rebuking of Judaism's *religio licita* by Tiberius and strictly enforced by Nero. To the emperors it seem easiest to revoke religious freedoms in the wake of Judaea's constant revolting rather than to adapt the entire empire's way of governing in appeasement to the insignificant province. The rebuke of Jewish religious freedom, in turn, cause even more rebellion due to the Roman's now being able to impose their own religious practices without a legal capacity – namely the worship of the emperor as an idol. One which Caligula reforms in drastic fashion by the placing of his image on the bodies of all godly statues.

In the year 66 CE the built up grievances of the Judeao-Romans under Rome's idolatry peaks as the empire refuses to act against the Syrians in Caesarea who sacrifice false offerings in front of the Jewish synagogue. This was allowed due to those inhabitants deemed stubborn by having their rights annulled in light of the leaders of Syrians at Caesarea ("Sadducees") offering substantial bribes to their Roman state for favor over their opposers. As a result the state sides with the "Greco-Hebrews" over the antiquated Hebrews in refusing to punish the Greco-Hebrews for their idolatrous sacrificing (no different than the historical Sadducee over the Pharisee; the heretic state of Judaea over the Jewish people in practice). By the empire's refusal to act, the Jewish people retaliate in attacking and killing Roman citizens and troops located in Jerusalem. With a direct response to retaliation, the Jewish leader

Agrippa II and his sister Berenice retreat north to the region of Galilee to remain in the graces of their Roman overseers – subsequently sending troops to assist the Roman's in squashing civil quarrels. It was at this point when the Sadducee-based Sanhedrin begins to converge itself with the imperial cult of Rome against the divergence of the antiquated Pharisee.

The uprising and killing of Roman soldiers calls for the emperor, Nero, to send his legate of Syria into the Holy Land and crush the rebellion outright. The Roman legate of Syria, general Cestius Gallus, marches toward Jerusalem through the by-pass city known as Beth Horon where the Roman's are ambushed and forced to retreat to the city of Antioch. Considered a major success to the Judaeo-Romans, the outcome of the Battle at Beth Horon influences the differing sects of Judaism to invest their lot with those who had rebelled – the Pharisaic Zealots. For their rebellion ignite what are known as the Jewish wars with Rome.

Upon Cestius Gallus' defeat, emperor Nero sends the renowned general known as Vespasian Flavius to crush the Jewish rebellion utterly.

The success at Beth Horon, however, allows the Zealot-led establishment of what is known as the (short lived) Judaean Free Government. Under this government, Roman-Judaea became occupied by antiquated Hebrews who choose for themselves to appoint Zealot leadership over designated regions. One Pharisaic Zealot named Yosef ben Matityahu, son of Matthias, is appointed commander over the territory of Galilee – the region where commander Vespasian begins his suppression.

It is important to note that during the short-lived reign of the Judaean Free Government there began an even more internal strife amongst the Hebrew people. This time between the Zealots and the Sicarii, the Sicarii being the radical function of the Zealots themselves. Where the Zealot is the radical to the Pharisee so is the Sicarii radical to the Zealot.

In the year 67 CE, Vespasian successfully besieges a Galilean city known as Yodfat. Under this besieging he is met by a Pharisaic Zealot who had surrendered to the Romans in contrast to his Jewish brethren committing suicide. This Zealot, the regional commanding appointed Yosef ben Matityahu, ultimately becomes the famed Titus Flavius Josephus after first surrendering unto Vespasian and later professing Vespasian as being *the* chosen messiah sent by Yahweh to re-teach the divine consequence of false worship. It is by the word of Josephus, the "commanding Zealot" of Galilee, by which Vespasian fulfills the prefigurement of *Immanuel* in relieving the chosen people from their idolatrous tendencies in not *fearing the Lord.* For the *Lord* Himself, via Vespasian, has been sent to cleanse Mankind, namely the once "chosen people," for His recurring wickedness .

The foretold prophecy of Josephus calls for Josephus himself to be a self-proclaimed Jewish prophet in the eyes of Vespasian (and therefore Rome). This self-proclamation of prophetic blessing is not unique to Josephus, however had existed within the rebellious province of Judaea long since Rome's first imperial birth under Augustus. One such false prophet is known as Judas the Galilean, the founder of the Zealot faction or "the fourth philosophy" (the other three being the Sadducee, Pharisee, and the Essenes). This Judas is perhaps best known for his role in leading a revolt against the Roman-imposed census of the year 6 CE under the Syrian legate Quirinius. Considered the founder of the "radical Pharisee" Judas betrays his Jewish brethren by encouraging the people to either defy Rome in refusing to register or face the threat of having their houses burned or property damaged (namely the theft of cattle). As a result, the Pharisaic Zealots had established their rebelliousness in the wake of the Julio-Claudians. Only for the two sons of Judas, named Simon (*Peter*) and James, to be later crucified under the reign of Nero and his Jewish-born procurator Tiberius Julius Alexander (nephew of the philosopher *Philo* of Alexandria) for their Zealot heresy in the eyes of Nero's Rome.

Once Josephus convinces Vespasian of his divine exaltedness (by way of the Cyrus-based messianic prophecies of antiquity) he is recruited by the Romans to act as a negotiating intermediary between the Jewish people and their Roman oppressors. With the civil state of Judaea already in shambles, Josephus contributes little in convincing the Roman's to spare the province from destruction. As Vespasian seeks to allow the state to destroy itself from the inside out, he is interrupted by his becoming emperor in the year 69 CE – where Josephus becomes looked upon with prophetic adoration for his previous professions. Due to his emperorship, Vespasian leaves his son Titus in charge to replace his command. However, Titus, unlike his father, sought not to wait for the rebellious Hebrews to destroy themselves. For he saw it best to end the rebellion once and for all by destroying the Second Temple in the year 70 CE at the Siege of Jerusalem. It is by this sieging and seizing of the Holy City that calls for the wealthy treasures of the Hebrew people to be taken from Jerusalem and back into Rome. A commemoration boasted by the still-standing Arch of Titus, celebrating the victories of the father-son dynasty of Vespasian and Titus.

The emperorship of Vespasian is symbolic to that of Augustus in the wake of Julius Caesar – with Nero symbolizing the latter. Both Vespasian and Augustus were placed into a position to ultimately restore Rome after the city's disunity under previous tyrannical leaders. These restoration efforts would align the emperor's leadership (and therefore *genius*) with the prosperity of the Roman state itself. So forth that any patriotic praise for the city was subliminally rendered unto the emperor at hand. For it was Nero who had selfishly constructed his own personal palace (the *Domus Aurea* i.e., "Golden House") at the expense of Rome's destruction in the Great Fire of Rome. An act which had separated the emperor from the people, best emphasized by the *Colossus of Nero* – a thirty-meter-high statue which idolized the emperor as the sole god. Only for Vespasian to usurp this personal house of emperor by building atop its foundations the *Flavian Amphitheater,* best known as the Roman Colosseum. An act of usurpation which had reunited the emperor with the people, for the purpose of this amphitheater was to serve the people (via entertainment). Entertainment by the basis of performances which represent the microcosmic form of Rome's macrocosmic ethos (that of imperialistic savagery) as represented through the gladiatorial games.

The foundation of the Colosseum's construction is founded on the grounds of Nero's idolatry and funded by the opulence of Judaean spoils. Where an inscription once read: "The Emperor Vespasian ordered [the *Flavian Amphitheater*] to be constructed from his share of the booty." Booty being the treasures carried from Judah to Rome after the Second Temple's destruction. Not only this, but the once-hailed *Colossus of Nero* is then renamed the *Colossus of Solis* after the emperor Vespasian's choice to add a crown of thorns to the idol's head – analogous to being "sun rays" gleaming from the head of Sol, the Roman sun god who now replaces the megalithic statue's idol imagery.

Thanks to their dynastic conquests in Judaea, Titus is able to utilize the prophetic blessings of the Jewish Zealot Josephus to deify his father Vespasian, he who had restored Rome by his building of the *People's Palace* (that being the Colosseum). Similar to Augustus in his deifying of Julius Caesar as being from the house of *Mars*, Titus deifies his father synonymously with the Hebrew house of *Yahweh*, for both Mars and Yahweh exist as redacted forms of the Babylonian god of war in Marduk. Choosing to be from the house of the "god of war" corroborates with the implied praise of successful conquests. An implied praise which is later exalted by the word *evangelium* (Latin for "*gospel*") meaning "*good news*" of military conquest. Where the newfound state of Rome's prosperity is brought back by Vespasian thanks to the gospel(s) of his conquest which had first began by the Sea of Galilee.

The difference between the Julio-Claudians (Julius Caesar to Augustus) and the Flavians (Vespasian to Titus) stem from the authentic paternity of each succeeding ruler. For Augustus, true, was *divi filius* to that of the godly Caesar except by adoptive (and therefore *earthly*) choosing. Titus, however, was the true son of Vespasian Flavius in that his paternity was not by adoptive (and therefore *non-earthly*) choosing but was genetic in predisposition. In that Augustus wasn't a *true son of god* in comparison to Titus, thus distinguishing the two. The pureness of such paternal heritage allow Titus, and therefore the entirety of his dynastic family, to separate their imperial holiness from the previous Julio-Claudians. For it was the decadence of Nero, as an ambassador for the Caesarian *genius,* who had relished in his power over the people until later reciprocated by the pleasantries of Vespasian and his aligning power *with* the people.

The congruency of the differing dynasties is met by their utilization of the *imperial cult*. First utilized by Alexander and later the Caesars, the imperial cult of Rome was now under the guidance of a "*Yahwistic*" ideal of worship – as professed by the Hebrew himself (i.e., Titus Flavius Josephus).

As previously mentioned, the introduction of a completely new god into the Roman pantheon was not uncommon. For the imperialistic Roman religion itself is based in Greek tradition, as evidenced by the architectural integrity of the Colosseum's construct. One such newfound god was during the time of Ptolemy I in Egypt with that of **Serapis Christus**, an intended god to bridge the Greek customs of Alexander's empire with that of the antiquated Egyptians. It was also during this time in which the Greek translation of the Hebrew TNK took place in the coining of the *Septuagint*. The newfound god named **Serapis Christus** was an invention by Ptolemy to infuse the already established Egyptian cult of Serapis (Osiris plus Apis, the sacred bull) with that of the Greek messiah in Christus (i.e., Ptolemy himself by the *genius* of Dionysus). As a result, the cult of **Serapis Christus** was formed by Ptolemy in order to fuse the Greek culture with that of the Egyptian.

Therefore, it is by the Flavians in which the implementation of Yahweh into the Roman pantheon emerges by way of imperialistic worship. This imperial worship of *Yahweh via Vespasian* is no different than that of the subliminal Caesarian *genius*. The only difference lay within the pureness of paternity in successive rule, where the Flavian dynasty is holy in comparison to the impurity of the Julio-Claudians. So forth that the imperial reign of the Caesarian *genius* is marked as *years of misguidance*. In the same light as *those* under the kingship of David and Solomon in comparison to those not – reminded by *those Yahwists* against *those Elohists*. Only now the kingship of heaven has been transferred out of the hands of the Hebrew and into the heart of the gentile.

For if the Flavians are to adopt the culture of Yahweh, they in turn must adopt the culture of the Hebrew. That is, unless, Yahweh's covenant is shifted. Shifted from the ways of days past (as symbolized by the TNK) and into a new testimony of faith over practice. Seeing as the Temple had been destroyed yet again, the idea between *earthly worship* and *heavenly guidance* are severed by the subjectiveness of practice. First between the Sadducees and Pharisees, the former favoring *earthly worship* over *heavenly guidance* – best exemplified by the dichotomy of Moses at Sinai. Later between the Greco-Hebrew and the antiquated Hebrew; where the latter falls in a mass diaspora due to their god's vindication. As a result, the favor of *earthly worship* surpasses the guidance of *spiritual antiquity,* for even the oral practices of Judaism are forced to be written down in the creation of the Mishnah and later the Talmud.

Now that favor has been shifted from the hands of the Hebrew, the welcoming of the gentile takes place in thanks to the imperial cult of Rome. These welcoming of the gentile is best expressed through the letters of Paul in his attempt to sway Hellenized cities to accept the newfound form of Judaism in Christianity. However, this form of early Christianity is marred by the underlying praise of *earthly* worship over *divine* submission; the former now represented by the *Flavian genius* in reciprocation to the once *Caesar.* The subjective interpretation of "how to practice" this newfound form of Judaism became distinguished between two factions yet again: the Flavian cult whom worship the *christus* (messiah) of the dynasty as an *actual being* versus the gnostic Hebrew who accepts their condemnation from *Yahweh via Vespasian* as an *allegory* ("Proverb") of teaching where the messiah is *not an actual being.*

Idol worship versus non-idol worship. Subjective heresy versus subjective non-heresy.

The reoccurring theme of Our introspective odyssey – an idealized *yin* and *yang* in the sense of *good* versus *evil.* The duality of existence against the non: creation versus destruction, only for *order* to emerge as the meaningful result of its mode-like median.

This duality is met by the social macrocosm of the Roman versus the Hebrew (relative to themselves). Only for the microcosm to reveal itself as the *heretical* Hebrew against the *non* (for the Roman's themselves are deemed heretics outright by the basis of their non-Jewishness). The overall impact of this duality results in the dichotomy between those Hebrews who worship the newfound *christus* (*Yahweh via Vespasian/Titus*) as an actual being or as an allegorical figure meant to teach the lesson of false worship (not maintaining a *fear of the Lord*). Those who bask in idolatry are backed by the *Flavian* imperial cult itself in their attempt to strip the Jewish-based customs of Judaism, namely their strict dietary laws and practice of *circumcision.*

The duality of the gnostic Hebrew versus the antiquated Hebrew is best represented by the differences between James the Just and Paul the Apostle. It was James, the supposed brother of Jesus, who taught the strict adherence to traditional Mosaic laws (i.e., dietary and circumcision) in that One must first become a Jew in order to practice Christianity. Meanwhile, Paul the Apostle sought to preach that, due to Christianity being a *physical* worshipping form of Judaism, the cultural acts of Mosaic antiquity were *not physically* required so forth One worshiped the *physical* form of *Yahweh via Vespasian/Titus.*

This duality is further rendered by the microcosmic allegory towards the traditional Jewish practice of *Yom Kippur,* the annual blood oath, where two identical goats are sacrificed on the basis of their symbolism between both *physical* and *spiritual.* The *physical* goat, the scapegoat, would have all of the sins of Israel cast upon it as it is first ran out into the wilderness and eventually chased off a cliff. This form of blood sacrifice is meant to represent the goat that "carries sin" against the second goat, the *spiritual* goat, whom is sacrificed with dignity in a pious ritual directly toward Yahweh. The *spiritual* blood sacrifice alludes to a "sinless" sacrifice offered to Yahweh in juxtaposition to the "sin-filled" sacrifice of the *physical.* Where, again, the notion of *good* versus *evil* is portrayed on the subjective nature of practicality. One could even understand how the newfound story of the trial between *Jesus and Barabbas* ("Barabbas" meaning "the son of the father" in Aramaic) where both characters act as varying forms of "the son of father" in Barabbas being the "sin-filled" sacrifice (who is **not chosen**) against Jesus being the "sinless" sacrifice (who is then **chosen**). The son of sinful Man against the son of sinless Yahweh (*via Vespasian,* i.e., Titus).

It is by the word of Paul which separates the gnostic "Hebrew" (i.e. Christian) from the antiquated Hebrew. The gnostic Hebrew, the Christian, need only to accept the *christus* as their idolized god for his *spiritual* teaching reign supreme. Whose spiritual teaching seems to further contradict the foundation of Judaism' tenets, primarily the idea of faith over practice (i.e., *Ecclesia* over *Synagoga*). The faith of Judaism depended on the practical efforts of the Jewish people to maintain their *fear of the Lord.* However, due to their lack of maintenance, the reciprocation of communication takes place in effort to "cleanse the wickedness" of Judaism by shifting faith (*spiritual*) without dependence on practice (*physical*). For the spiritual is now accounted for by virtue of the *christus'* physical being of practical sacrifice.

It was within the entirety of antiquated Jewish customs that cause for their corruptive downfall. This is best expressed by the meaning of Paul's letters, which further reveals the duality of nature within its form. The formation of which categorizes *those* letters that represent the *external* obligations of the church (how to behave as a Christian *outside* of church) against *those* epistles which articulate the *internal* affairs of the church (how One must behave within the church itself). The *external* letters are known as those letters sent to cities (Romans, Galatians, Corinthians, etc.) while the *internal* letters are those sent to actual Men (known as the Pastoral Epistles). Those Men being *Titus* and *Timothy*; one who represents the tough Roman against the other being a timid Hebrew. For it was *Timothy* who was circumcised while *Titus* was not. For it was *Timothy* who yearned for both guidance and instruction from Paul while *Titus* need only instruction. For it was *Timothy* who represented the antiquated Hebrew while *Titus* alludes to the gentile convert. Where the antiquated Hebrew knew the word of ancient scripture in contrast to the new, while the gentile convert knew nothing of antiquity and therefore transitions with ease. In that the antiquated Hebrew need more "convincing of *christus*" for they understood the implications of Christianity's reciprocation in contrast to Jewish antiquity. Therefore, the timidness of Timothy adheres to the dichotomy between himself and Titus the tough gentile convert. However, it is within the letter(s) to Timothy in which Paul articulates the assurance of quality upkeep within the church's *leadership* while Titus's epistle explains the upkeep of *membership*. A further revelation of reciprocation by way of each's practical importance.

Yin and yang. Alpha and beta. Good and evil. *Us* and *them*.

Once the Flavian dynasty falls, as too does Rome as a sustainable empire. For the title of *emperor* became meaningless as the emperorship became usurped by the godliness of Vespasian and his paternal successors – no different than that of the cult of Amun against the Pharaoh of Egypt's New Kingdom. Where the ruler (then *Caesar*) was no longer a god for god himself (i.e., *Yahweh via Vespasian*) was now king. Subject only to the word of *His* intermediaries, that being the *Flavian* imperial cult.

After what became known as the "era of the good emperor's" (post *Flavian* dynasty), Rome begins to fall into disarray. So forth that the Empire becomes split into four factions under the reign of emperor Diocletian, he who persecutes the Christian church (before it was truly a church). The underlying practice of early Christianity being met by persecution came under non-Flavian emperorship, those who had no need of upkeep with the Judaeo-Roman people (shifting the *Flavian* imperial cult into the later *Nervine-Antonine* and *Severan*). These persecutions remain ongoing until the eventual rise of Constantine the Great – he who sought to restore the four factions of Rome as one.

No different than that of Julius Caesar to Augustus and later Vespasian over Nero, there exists a common theme of the state of Rome being brought into pious order from previous disorderly chaos. Having centuries of redacted perfection to learn from, Constantine is able to reshape the failing Roman state by way of his aligning himself with *the people*. First with Augustus in his subliminal praise of adoration; second with Vespasian in the blending of Judaeo-Roman values (namely with his introduction of favor for the gentile). Once Vespasian had introduced Yahweh (*via* himself) into the Roman pantheon, the traditional Roman began to refuse the piety of an unforeseen god otherwise useless to their cultural existence. In response to such heresy, the conservative Diocletian enforces the purging of external paganism (namely the cult of *christus*). It was then Saint Constantine who, by the jurisdiction of successful conquests, reunites the empire in the reciprocation of exaltation. In exalting the cult of *christus* and rendering himself the implementer of the church; the groom of the bride. Where the warrior-king as *christus* liberates those being oppressed, beginning with those Hebrews under the evil Nebuchadnezzar and later with those Christians under the dominion of Diocletian. Due to Constantine's messianic liberation efforts, he sought to invest his *genius* with that of both Augustus and the Flavian's in retaining the praenomen *Flavius* and incorporating the adoptive cognomen of *Augustus.* This investment allows Constantine to adopt both the (perceived) *earthly* omnipotence of Caesar <u>and</u> the *spiritual* omnipresence of Yahweh (*via Vespasian*). As a result, Constantine adopts what is known as the long-held *ceasaropapism*: that which unifies the church with the state – making Constantine the bridegroom of a christened Rome. Another self-proclaimed *philosopher-king* of the Western-world: the *wise lord* Himself.

The entirety of Constantine's *christus* adoption calls for those who accept Constantine as the emperor <u>and</u> Pontifex Maximus from those who do not. This distinction, one that parallels the dichotomy of the gnostic Hebrew from the antiquated, is further brought to light in sight of the Arian Controversy. The "Arian Controversy" was one which analyzed the holy trinity of the *father, the son,* and *holy spirit* as being all in one or one within all. The former reveals the trinity as being co-eternal amongst both the *father* and *son* (guided by the *holy spirit*), while the latter explains them all as being separate in their likeliness. If god is the father however not the son, then the holiness of Constantine as a bridegroom is nullified. Only by god being both the *father* and the *son* (via the *holy spirit*) can Constantine uphold his caesaropapism – justifying the state's exercising of power and expansion as a edict from "god Himself" (via the emperor). As a result, the paganism of the Roman pantheon (one which justifies successful conquest by expansion) infuses itself with the cultural traditions of Judaism without its obligatory requirements of conversion.

It is within the religious jurisdiction of Judaism's Abrahamic literature when coupled by the excuse for wrath by conquest in which Islam becomes founded. However, founded in reciprocation to the *bridegoom*ness of the chosen *christus*. For the next would be one chosen without the implied blasphemy of Man being Himself co-eternal with Allah ("Allah" being Arabic for "God"). Only within the idolatrous nature of image-worship does Man bend to the whim of evil (via ignorance), first expressed by the Jewish people themselves and later by the Roman Empire. Therefore, worship of the coming messiah should depend not on His image (for Allah himself is *unseen*) but on the grander of *goodness* (via *wisdom*) in His actions (via conquest). For the true prophet, may His soul rest eternally in peace, understood His role as the soul representative of Mankind's potential philosopher-king: He who unifies the state of existence by way of His prophetic *wisdom*.

Religion

Have You heard the good news?

It is by the good word of the Persian *Saoshyant* (i.e. *Savior*) named Cyrus in which the absolving of Mankind's earthly ignorance (by way of liberating oppression) occurs for the ancient Jewish people. The reason for such universal kindness originates from the core of their religious culture in Zoroastrianism.

Natively known as *Mazdayasna*, the Greek form "Zoroastrianism" retains its name from the acclaimed prophet known as Zarathustra ("Zoroaster" in Greek), He who spoke the good word of *wisdom*. Thusly, by His word, absolves the ignorance of Man's mortal predisposition: that of finite existence.

The fundamental difference between any Man and His god is the distinction of quality between the *mortal* and *immortal* – One who is bound by *time* and the other who is not. One who experiences *time* in a linear fashion in contrast to the other's experience being cyclical (by its immortal unlimitedness). One of definitiveness in His own existence while the other reigns supremely indefinite; separated only by pious transcendence.

The dual nature of Nature itself – the paradox between the *alpha* and *beta*. Where the god(s) themselves accumulate as alpha, only for the mortal to behave as beta.

To understand Zarathustra and the importance of his teachings, One must first revisit the testament of his objective origins. Though conventionally dated around the very time of Ahmosis' mass exodus (c. 1500 BCE), the esoteric core of Zoroastrianism (that being the dual nature of Nature) exists much earlier. The name *Zarathustra* itself connotes not any one person in particular but exemplifies an allegorical representative as the *first named individual* who contrasts newfound beliefs against the old. For the title *Zarathustra* is thought to translate as "The Golden Double Shining Star" where each word in *zar-tu-ush-stra* retains its respective meaning. Whose name in whole, by way of its *double* or dual nature, exalts two shines to one star – i.e., two sides to one coin.

Alpha and beta in congruence to existence. Where existence, which precedes Life, acts as the alpha to Life being the beta. The distinction between inorganic and organic matter; that which is confined by the entropic nature of *time* and that which is not. That which possesses qualities of conscientiousness in contrast to that which is idle.

Idle by insentience – ignorant to *time's* physically damning existence.

To live is to exist even though existing doesn't assure living. As a result, existence precedes Life and is therefore *alpha* to Life being *beta*. The duality of Nature itself (via *alpha* and *beta*) act as a microcosmic allegory for the macrocosm in *existence* against *non-existence: physical* against *spiritual*.

Earthly worship vs. spiritual acquiescence – the separation between *spirituality* and the *physical* state.

Consciousness vs. *unconsciousness* – the dichotomy between the *earthly* body and the *spiritual* mind.

Objectivity vs *subjectivity* – the notion of *pure* judgement against *impure* bias.

Time vs. *space* – the designation of *when* against *where* (with respect to any given *who*).

Understanding this core belief of Nature's duel allows the further comprehension of what it means to be a Human Being, One stricken with the <u>human condition</u>. For We are all apart of a single race – the Human race. Embrace the irrefutable nature of what it means to be alive an endowed with self-awareness, a quality distinct to those who are *aware* of their own ignorance in contrast to those *unaware*.

The separation between *wisdom* and ignorance exists only in their reciprocation of one another in function. The former is guided by *truth* and *love* while the latter is led by *deceit* and *intentional misguidance* – both gaining knowledge in their respective fields. One gains the knowledge of ignorance as being bliss (by using its manifestation for personal advantage) while the other shuns the impure fallibility of ignorance outright.

In the eyes of Zarathustra, his teachings act as an inclusive critique of his fellow Man in an attempt to separate *them* against *us* in that, though separate, *us* and *them* are still of the same single coin. That which differentiates the two sides stems from the mind-set of the individual with respect to their conceptualization of *time* – that being *linear* against the otherwise *cyclical*.

Those who view *time* as *cyclical* are seen as those who understand their gods to be innately capricious in unpredictability by taking form of natural phenomena (though One would expect their *cyclicality* to produce predictability). For if the gods are equivalent to the forces of Nature, then they are in turn associated with Her omnipresent qualities. One quality in particular is the cyclical form of the sun's eternal appearance in its 365 day journey of cosmic fulfillment. First from the birth of its eternal sunshine (marked by the winter solstice) to its full circling of degradation at the turn of the summer solstice. The perception of *time* as being *cyclical* is due to Nature's recurring seasonality.

For it is true, seasonality (a subjective quality of Nature) is cyclical as a *physical* manifestation. However, *time,* as spoken by Zarathustra, is experienced not by recurring cycles but by an ever-present notion of eternal progress. It is only within the cosmic origins between being *objective* or *subjective* in which distinguishing cyclicality from linearity occurs. Where, objectively speaking, *time* becomes no different than that of *space* itself, connoting the two as being not in separation but unified as one.

Two sides of the same coin of existence – alluding to the notion of a singular *spacetime* continuum.

(think on this)

To firmly comprehend the significance of Zarathustra's reformation, One must revisit its objective origins. Before the establishment of agrarian societies, Mankind was known for His nomadic ways in the sense that being *nomadic* came first – before that of the *agrarian settler.* Synonymous to *us* against *them,* the nomad is considered *alpha* in chronological existence when compared to the agrarian settler being the *beta.* The dualistic intricacies of the *nomad* against the *settler* is the underlying theme behind many famous fables, namely *Cain* versus *Abel,* the sufferer of possession against the righteous wanderer. Cain, whose name reflects the Hebrew word in *kana* meaning "to possess" while Abel's title retains the *alpha* and *beta* qualities of *El* himself.

It is Yahweh who rejects Cain for his agrarian ways while accepting the ability of Abel's agility. For the agrarian ways (i.e., the way of society) depends on trade and materialistic praise. Only by the attraction of idol craftsmanship does the farmer exchange his produce via trade – where the ingenuity of craftsmanship (*spiritual* imagination via *creation*) overthrows the practicality of physical farming. Where the adoration for the *physical* topples the appreciation of the *spiritual*. In such a sense, the improvement of imaginative thought grants separation for *us the thinkers* against *those in practice*. Where *those in practice* depend on the superficiality of societal existence (via materialism, thanks to trade) to achieve **contentment** while *us, those who think,* need only the knowledge of *wisdom* to thrive.

Wisdom in the sense of One's self-awareness amidst ignorance's indefinite exaltation. Where knowledge acts as alpha via *wisdom* (and is therefore *objective*) while the beta form of knowledge reigns in subjective ignorance via arrogance.

However, One cannot physically *live* and prosper as an existing being without materialistic dependence – especially post-nomadicism. This materialistic dependence is grounded within the nourishment of food and water; food further symbolizing the *physical* against the *spiritual* being water. As a result, any and all who exist depend on the nourishment of themselves at the expense of another's. Where the act of *physically* eating (the *creation* of nourishment for Oneself) is met only in direct reciprocation to the physical destruction of fellow living beings (whether it be animal or plant). It is within only the spiritual acquiescence of *drinking* (water) where nutritious *creation* emerges from the expanse of nothingness.

Cain, though a beta, is considered *physically* superior to that of Abel in the sense that agriculture produces more surplus of physical food (though at the expense of the land's fertility) in comparison to the humility of the herdsman. In contrast, it is Cain who is considered *spiritually* inferior to that of Abel, he who is alpha with respect to his *nomadic wisdom*.

These qualities of Cain and Abel articulate the core principle behind Zarathustra's teachings within the Abrahamic scripture. However, long before the Hebrews emerge as a designated people, the Sumerians had already established this dichotomy between the *righteous wanderer* and the beta *agrarian* in the tale of the Gilgamesh epic, known as the world's first *written* story. For it is within the "Epic of Gilgamesh" (c. 2600 – 2000 BCE) in which the warrior-king named Gilgamesh, born one-third Human and two-thirds divine, reciprocates the secondarily mentioned "wild-Man" named Enkidu – he who is two-thirds Human and one-third divine. The intention of each character's motif parallels directly to that of Cain and Abel; Gilgamesh reigning as the societal settler in the wake of Enkidu's birth from the wilderness.

The title *Gilgamesh* itself translates as "the elder/authority [being] a young man" which is intended to allude to the *beta*ness of agriculture (society being "the younger") as being the authoritative usurper of the original nomadic alpha. No different than that of the son in his dethroning of the father – for the elder is now a young man. As a result, there exists a reciprocation of transmutation between the qualities of *alpha* and *beta* and their practical function. Where the beta is *physically* the *alpha* and the alpha is *physically* the *beta*. Only within their *spiritual* qualities do they exist as their own.

A duality of reciprocation by the being of below or as above. That which is below, or *beta* to the above *alpha*, retains its authentic function only in its *spiritual* existence. In the sense that the physical existence of Gilgamesh is superior only by earthly parameters while the *wisdom* of Enkidu transcends their earthly form.

For it is Gilgamesh who represents the Sumerian pantheon as their *physical* emanation (being two-thirds divine) while Enkidu embodies the pantheon's *spiritual* guidance (being two-thirds Human). The "powerfully built hero" against "he who lives in the wild." One who resembles a pattern of physical strength against the other who acts with spiritual guidance.

The Epic of Gilgamesh contrasts Cain and Abel in its convergence of Enkidu and Gilgamesh as a divine pair rather than an act of divergence. Instead of Cain choosing to kill Abel, it was by the choice of the Sumerian pantheon to mark Enkidu and not Gilgamesh with death (as a result of the two's naïve waywardness in their attempted journey to reach the gods). Only for the death of Enkidu to cause for Gilgamesh's sorrow, for he had not questioned the mortality of himself until the death of his "other-half." If Enkidu was marked by death, so too must Gilgamesh, who then denounces his *physical* awesomeness in the wanting to reclaim the image of his lost brother. By denouncing his "fate" (for he was destined to be a physical feat), Gilgamesh grieves in honor of his brother by roaming the wild in search for *wisdom* – *wisdom* in attaining an everlasting Life of mortality. Though still one-third Human, the mortal predisposition of Gilgamesh isn't fully grasped until the death of his divine brother. In his quest for *truth*, after first reaching the Road of the Sun and following its path for "twelve *double* hours," Gilgamesh encounters the post-flood survivor in *Ziusudra* (later named Utnapishtim and eventually Atra-Hasis). This *Ziusudra* of Sharrupak, as mentioned in *Subchapter 3*, is the last king of Sumer (before the grand deluge) whose name translates as being "Life of long days." Once Sargon and his ethnic Akkadians usurp the Sumerian people, so too does their implementing of Akkadian epithets onto Sumerian gods and heroes. From *Ziusudra* to *Utnapishtim*; from he who brought the "Life of long days" to the new "He [who] founded Life." Similarly, once Hammurabi's Babylonians overthrow the Akkadians, so too does their designation of renaming. Whose renaming of *Utnapishtim* becomes the renowned *Atra-Hasis,* a name rendering as the "extremely wise." All in all, the *three names* of Ziusudra/Utnapishtim/Atra-Hasis all represent the same traditional post-flood hero (synonymous with Noah) whose generational lineage account for a newfound form of Mankind: he who found the Life of long days by his extremely wise guidance.

The *Life of long days* act as an allegory for a post-flood Mankind who has become self-aware of Himself by the basis of extreme *wisdom*. Where *wisdom* grants intuition and inevitably assures an evolution of intellectual growth. Growth with accounts for the improvement of diet, meal preparation, and eventually medicine. Intellectual intervention, granted by *wisdom,* that extends the longevity of Life as a living being.

But is this *wisdom* new? From where does this *wisdom* stem?

From a cyclic standpoint, the birthplace of *wisdom* is unknown – seeming to appear simply as an edict from the gods. However, from the perspective of Zarathustra, a linear revelation reveals *wisdom* as the ever-present quality within the paternity of *time*. As *time* increases, so does *wisdom*. As Man's *time* on earth (in existence) increases, so too does His *wisdom* in dealing with His mortal defiance.

The entirety of Zoroastrianism itself acts as the earliest form of monotheism against traditional polytheism. Once the Ice Age came to an end, a severance occurred between those who wandered and settled versus those who *kept wandering*. Those who settled became agrarian farmers, content in their settlement, while those who kept wandering remain forever on the move. From an idealistic perspective, those who "settle" seem content by their immobility. Contrastingly, those who *keep wandering* seem to fulfill a never-ending journey of journeying until the day of their death. Hence, the notion between the cyclical perspective of the farmer (which depends on the objective understanding of the otherwise subjective seasonality) against the progressive mindset of the ever-wandering wanderer. The intricacies of maintaining any agrarian society depends first on the preservation of knowledge and secondarily on the documentation of ideals. The former, which both the agrarian and wanderer agree, objectively contributes to the growth of *wisdom* over *time*. It is within the perspective of documentation from which the dichotomy of the wanderer from the settler takes form. The duel between *oral* tradition and *written* practice; the barbaric tradition of retaining knowledge against a newfound form of civilized practice.

This is best exemplified by the migration of a people known as the Indo-Iranians. These Indo-Iranian nomads considered themselves to be "Aryan" from the Sanskrit word *arya* meaning "noble." The modern misinterpretation of the "Aryan race" derives its origins from Northern Middle-Eastern roots – that being from the Caucasus mountains near the Caspian Steppe. For it were these Indo-Iranian nomads who venture from the north and eventually part ways depending on *those who settled* versus those who did not. Those who settle do so at the expense of whatever indigenous people are already living in the lands, a common characteristic for imperial pioneers. Those indigenous settlers, separate from societal settlers, became known as the *sudras* in contrast to the conquering *aryans* of nobility.

The sudra sheep herder versus the aristocratic aryan.

This dual existence inevitably manifests itself as the distinction between the languages of *Vedic Sanskrit* and *Gathic Avestan* – sister languages of a distant mother language. Two sides of a common linguistic coin, whose mother language coincides with a common culture of antiquity.

The differences between Sanskrit and Avestan exists not in their likeliness by language but by contrasts in culture. The language of the two are eerily similar in that they share an abundant amount of grammatical concepts, differing only in word meanings due to phonetic change (or *sound* shift). Where the *sound* shift occurs, many *words* themselves retain their physical appearance in spelling and apparent pronunciation. It is within the *meaning* of the words themselves does an implied reciprocation occur, best expressed by the cultural meaning of the Sanskrit terms in *deva* and *asura* against the Avestan terms in *ahura* and *daeva*. Where the Avestan *ahura* alludes to the benevolent lords of divinity against the Sanskrit *asura* who represent the demonic gods of malevolence. Only for the Sanskrit *deva* to denote those proper gods of an Indic pantheon against the Avestan *daeva* who act as an abomination within the Gathas.

The Avestan *Gathas* ("gatha/gita" meaning "song/hymn" in both Sanskrit and Avestan) represent a proverbial reciprocation to the Sanskrit *Vedas*. No different than that of the shasu Hebrew against their newfound Canaanite opposers, the tradition of the former acts as an inclusive critique within their own culture milieu. The antiquated Hebrew sought to cleanse the idol-sewn ignorance of their fellow Man by distinguishing *their* abominable actions in light of "*our*" (the Hebrew's) gnostic teaching. Similarly, the Gathic teachings of Zarathustra were an open assessment against the otherwise established Vedic principles of antiquity. The former reveals a confounding concept of *true free will* against the orthodoxy of *determinism*. Where the Sanskrit culture revolves around *fate,* the Avestan culture is lineated by *choice*.

The foundation of Avestan Zoroastrian stands upon the idea of a singular, yet limited, god who engages in battle against his coeval; the spiritual emanation of evil itself (by way of *ignorance*) named Angra Mainyu. It is the god of above, that being Ahura Mazda (hence *Mazda*yasna), who is considered the eternal one of *wisdom* while Angra Mainyu besets below. The purpose of Mankind's existence is His ability to *choose,* here on earth (as One lives and breathes), to either contribute to *wisdom* or abide by *ignorance.* In the eye of a believer, One who submits themselves to *goodness* against the otherwise non contributes their being to the cosmic battle on the side of the *wise* – the predetermined *spiritual* winner by way of *physical* entropy.

Choosing right over wrong in **this Life.** Choosing to help One's fellow being or deciding to not. Choosing to contribute to the goodness of *wisdom* against the *ignorance* of idolatry.

Even though the strife of death seems subjectively wrong, the necessity for its presence is objectively essential. In order to attain appreciation, One must taste distain. In the sense that just as good and evil are of the same lot, so too are Life and death in relation to mortal existence. Where *Life* and *death* act as opposing faces on the coin of existence, so too does their macrocosmic function in relation to its microcosmic derivations. This can be easily understood by the qualities of the macrocosmic sun when compared to its artificial microcosm in controlled *fire.* As the sun acts with eternal light, warmth, security, and nourishment so too does Man's fire in allowing cooking for nourishment, wrath for security, limited warmth, and definitive light. One must know darkness to understand light. One must accept death in order to appreciate Life.

Only when the toddler touches the fire do they understand it's wrath. Only by staring directly into the sun does One become blind. Only by experiencing chaos does One become all the wiser.

Aside from *free will* versus *fate,* the most significant principle to note is the difference between *oral* and *written* tradition. To the older generations of Man (who considered themselves *alpha),* their existence knows only of spoken language. To them, language retains only its *spiritual* form in that words, sentences, and stories exist without being *physically* formed (via *documentation*). The practice of "what means *what*" derives from the **faith**

140

that any language's *spiritual* form (and therefore meaning) will be passed down from generation to generation without corruption.

Contrastingly, the newer generations who had discovered *written documentation* did so at the expense of *oral* tradition. In the sense of that which is *written* is marked in stone and unchanged by *time*. While the antiquity of oration reigns indefinitely changing in congruence with Man's own intellectual growth. Where the **faith** of *oral* tradition depends not on the unchanged form of *written documentation* but on the linear evolution of itself.

Thus, the elder in contrast to the young man; those who bask in the comfort of antiquity against those who seek to evolve with discomfort. Those who accept the ways of their own waywardness in light of those who accept progress. Those who accept idle virtues in the wake of those wanting change. For the elder is now the young man.

Again, the lingering quality of *reciprocation* exalts itself within the *physical* presence between *oral* and *written*. Oral tradition requires the physical presence of its audience while the written practice does not. Meaning the *oral* tradition itself is not physically existent without the intimate intermediary of some Man – only for the *written* word of any Men to remain timeless and without an intermediary. Where the spoken word can be analyzed in the presence of He who spoke while the written word is open to interpretation. So forth that the *written* is considered *non-malleable* while the *oral* is indefinitely *malleable* in congruence to its linear evolution.

To the elders, the notion of One "needing to *document* their *wisdom*" reveals the presence of **non-faith** in the passing of any Holy sermon. Why would One need to document their knowledge of *wisdom* if they possess **faith**? Surely **faith** in their teachings would be enough to assure the piety of any Holy word as remaining sanctified across the span of *time*. In a sense, *oral* tradition is dependent on **faith** while the *written* word alludes to not having **faith** in the face of *time's* progressiveness. For this would become the argumentative source in justifying the burning of libraries and destruction of historical literature. Acts of abomination, grounded by ignorance, resulting in the intellectual setback of unknown potential.

Cain versus Abel: he who requires both the sight and sound of the Holy word against he who needs only its sound. No different than that of timid *Timothy* against *Titus* the tough.

Therefore, Zarathustra's teachings distinguish the disparity of the *new* against the *old*, for the elder is now a young man. Whose teachings articulate the progressive form of *wisdom* against the cyclicality of ignorance. From a superficial perspective, the cyclicality of seasonality seems undying and never ending. Meanwhile, Man remains predisposed to mortal definitiveness – living a linear life with an inevitable end. Hence the dichotomy of the elder's teachings in light of the new, where existence, not just Life, promulgates linearity in the sense that *all things come to an end* (even the cyclicality of seasonality, i.e., its subjective *beta*-ness). For the Sun will eventually burnout (though seemingly "forever in the future") as the entropic nature of Nature itself radiates towards a singularity of despair. An assurance for an end to all that exists.

Thus, the revolution of Revelations – the coming to terms with One's own macrocosmic death. By understanding not only the mortality of One's individual self but that of Nature in its infinite entirety, the individual becomes humbled in knowing their mortality's irrelevance against Nature's malevolence. By One knowing they are no different than that of all else in existence allows an ease of relief to their subjective *ego*, exalting an elevated view of objective awareness. A true acceptance of the Universe's macrocosmic mortality as being so above to their own mortal predisposition – that which is seemingly below. Accepting the *fear of the Lord* is to come to terms with an end-all-be-all of all in existence as being inevitable.

Hence the eschatological entry of the *messianic prophecies* introduced into the Old Testament. Ones that began to take form post-Cyrus' liberation. A revelation of introspection, which rebirths an elevated awareness of objectivity in light of the *ego's* death.

For it is within the *wisdom* literature of Zarathustra's teachings in which the end of days is prophetically claimed. Where the final moments of mortal existence is met by a duel between lightness and darkness (i.e., good and evil, alpha and beta) in which the goodness of light prevails. The ultimate triumph of the alpha over the beta, the *spiritual* over the *physical*, as the physical Universe promulgates toward eternal darkness while the spiritual consciousness converges into a singularity of *wisdom*. The core principle within this profound ideal reveals the conundrum for physical existence needing to end at the indefinite expanse of spirituality's omnipresence. In that the only way for an individual to truly become pure and pious is to rid themselves of their physical state, for the mortality in meat degrades the host of omniscience. Perhaps this is why Enkidu was chosen over Gilgamesh to transcend the parameters of earthly existence.

Therefore, the end of days is seen as the macrocosmic continuation of One's own microcosmic fulfillment in their days as being. Fulfilling the daily battle of triumphing *goodness* over *ignorance* via the *wisdom* of self-awareness. One who is self-aware of the objectivity within *time's* linear progression against the otherwise subjective sense of cyclicality.

V) Islam – The Rebirth of Devotion

Wisdom, the ever-living master of eternity; there is no progress without Her.

The edict of Persian Zoroastrianism becomes long antiquated within the Middle East alongside Judaeo-Christianity during the times of tribal Arabia by the year 570 CE. The Arabian Peninsula as a whole is grounded as being the motherland of all Semitic languages.

The geographic bridge between Africa and Eurasia; acting as an intermediary between two sides of a single-known world. Primarily between the Egyptians and Sumerians, later with the Byzantines and Sassanids, and eventually amongst the twentieth century United States and Soviet Union. It is within the establishment of the indigenous Arabian people in which the rise of the Semites takes place. An upbringing of a "single people" that falls at a fault during migration; those who maintain their wandering against those who do not. Those who venture forth in progressive migration and those who remain in idle cyclicality.

The former establishes the "Eastern Semitic" sect while the latter remain within the peninsula as the western sect. *Those* Eastern Semites would eventually become known as the very Akkadians to challenge the Sumerians. Only for the Western Semites, who remain nomadic throughout their homeland, to eventually permeate the Levant and establish themselves (i.e., are best represented by) the legacy of the Phoenicians.

The problem with the Arab Peninsula is its rigid infertility, excluding its southern-most territories. In essence, Arabia exists as a vast geographic expanse of hardly habitable terrain, one impoverished of natural resources and lacking virtually any significant stream reservoirs. The dryness of the Arab plain forces its inhabitants to progressive nomadism; to either immigrate southward or emigrate towards the north. An edict from Nature in Her attempt to thwart a sect of Mankind from adopting the ways of settled cyclicality – best represented by the city of Mecca.

Until the rise of multicultural trade.

The perks of the arid Arab lands exist as being the middleman between many unknown worlds *all while* retaining an image of an infertile *undesirableness*; fearing not from the thought of external conquest (similar to ancient Egypt in its deserts acting as deterrents). Therefore, the indigenous tribes of old Arabia, best represented by the Bedouin, exist with relative prosperity during times of contemporary chaos.

The rise of multicultural trade allows the Arabian Peninsula to perfect its role as the merchant trade center of many unconnected people. With an import/export basis of reliability, the tribes of Arabia are able to sustain themselves throughout a region otherwise considered unsustainable. This is largely in thanks to the domestication of the camel by the year 1,000 BCE, which acts as the land ship in navigating the desert seas. No different than the domestication of the auroch, the camel reveals an intimate connection with its masters in playing a crucial role in the evolution of Ourselves. Though the auroch assumes a role within agriculture, the camel compels the desert nomad ever forward.

By the time the tribes of Arabia establish themselves they do so on the basis of tribal loyalties rather than a central government. Without a central civil institution, family and extended family are seen as the qualitative supplement for jurisdiction. In the sense of kinship being the foundation from which feuds were settled, most of which were grounded within the availability of water. The ruler of each tribe, later known as a *sheik*, rules with limited power. Each ruler is questionable by the basis of subordinate loyalty. The sheik themselves are seen as the settler of disputes – an arbiter as the tribal philosopher king. Though this role is that of the judge and the jury, the executioner aspect of the leader resides in his fulfillment of *ghazw* or *razzia* which is the expeditionary raids of other Arabian tribes. Raids which resulted in the desecration and conquest of fellow western nomadic pastoralists. The enabling of Cain-like qualities amongst Bedouin brethren – no different than the parting of blood-ties between the Yahwist and the Elohist.

Ghazw is seen as the survival of the fittest aspect within an arid tribal Lifestyle. No different than that of the farmer tilling the ground, the mounds of killing of men by Man express a notion of creation from destruction. Where the farmer creates surplus at the destruction of an area's fertility, the alpha tribe creates splendor at the expense of the beta's destruction. One must not look at the actions of another without an objective understanding of the other's intentions. Is a lion evil for creating nutrition for itself and its family at the expense of a gazelle's Life? Even though the gazelle had a family of its own, who loved and cared for its existence, is it wrong for Nature to allow such realities? The tribes of any ancient culture exist in the primitivism of survival of the fittest in which the physical alpha reigns supreme no matter the beta. Similar to a mother bear killing her own young, the burning sensation of survival at its fittest reveals the importance of *me* over *you*. The *me* encompasses multidimensional aspects from *first* the individual then the individual to the family, from the family to the tribe, and eventually from the tribe to the community. Each layer of the *me* represents the inclusion of the friend (good) over the exclusion of any foe (evil).

The *me* is always good while the *you* can be both. The *you* upholds either the companionship of the *me* or all of which is unsavory to the survival of the *me*. This idea of *you* in whole, from the perspective of the individual *me*, can either represent *you* the friend (good) or *you* the foe (evil). Where *me* the individual (Yourself as the reader) is seen as only a friend (i.e., the ego of the individual sees itself as holistically infallible) as opposed to any other individuals who are all open to interpretation. The friendly *you* is included alongside the *me* as a friend while the woeful *you* threatens prosperity. Whether it is *you* the individual or *you* the collective, the foe is perceived as nothing more than nutrition to feed selfish desires. In which the downfall of the foe fuels the fervor of the friend.

Such is the meaning for *ghazw* or *razzia* – originating from the Arabic word meaning "to want/raid." For the individual *me* to want and to possess the survival of Nature's game at the price of another's end. No different than the act of simply eating in its emergence of nutrition at the cost of organic destruction. The evolution of *me* at the death of thee.

The tribal raids amongst fellow Arabs eventually gives rise to the fittest. Generally, a title given to the Quraysh tribe, these mercantile tradesmen establish themselves as the controlling inhabitants of the city of Mecca – the renowned trade hub of the Arab Peninsula. The leaders of the city act as hospitable hosts to any and all guests; most of whom were polytheistic pilgrims who came to worship the Ka'aba.

The Ka'aba, known as the *sacred cube,* is a granite stone block worshipped by the indigenous Arabs synonymous to the Tabernacle of the Old Testament. The cube itself represents the house of Allah in its role as the physical manifestation of His presence. A presence so strong and sacred that various tribes from all over would venture forth to Mecca for an annual migration of worship. Not only this, but the traditions of Abraham (Judaism and Christianity) and Zoroastrianism were well understood and established at this point in *time.*

However, before the Ka'aba acts as the house of a single god (Allah) it is first revered as the house of all gods – acting as a generalized idol for any and all to worship.

A corruptive quality of idol imagery needing to transcend its original primitive meaning.

Similar to Yahweh sending David to unite the tribes of Israel, the prophet Muhammad is sent by god to unite the tribes of Arabia.

During the late sixth century CE the prophet Muhammad is born into a prominent Meccan mercantile family. As an idol tradesman, the young Muhammad lives amongst the polytheistic tribes of the time *for forty years* until he hears the word of Allah through the voice of the angel known as Gabriel. It is by this experience that elevates the Man as a prophet and the intermediary between the one true god and His people. An intermediary who is set to absolve the ignorance of polytheism in the wake of the one true god.

Islam means to submit to the *fear of the Lord,* and a Muslim is One who submits themselves to such fear. The intention of such submission lies congruent with the principles of its fellow Abrahamic traditions – namely in part of Judaism's practicality and secondarily on the proselytization of Christianity by way of its transferring Yahweh's favor from the Jew to the Gentile.

In the eyes of the ancient Arab, the wickedness of Yahweh's favor originally stems from choosing of Isaac over Ishmael. Similar to Cain versus Abel, Isaac represents the younger while Ishmael acts as the first-born. In which Ishmael represents the alpha wanderer against Isaac being the beta settler.

The intention of Islam is to critique the wickedness of its fellow religious sects – primarily with the idea of Christianity's idol worship of the *"son of god."* In the eyes of a believer, god represents the transcendental quality of consciousness (that which is *unseen*). The dichotomy between the Christian and the Muslim stems from their perception of god's elevated godliness. To the Christian, Jesus Christ represents the *actual son* of god. To the Muslim, Jesus Christ represents the prefigurement of Immanuel who is sent to absolve the ignorance of the believers at the time. For if the Christian believes in Jesus as an actual extension of god, then the Muslim is thought to perceive their views as polytheistic – no different than those contemporary polytheistic tribes. With this being said, Islam still considers Judaism and Christianity as "people of the book" and one of the same tradition (of Abraham). Only the previous two have been corrupted by the idol ways of days past.

In the eyes of Islam, Muhammad is seen as the messenger of god similar to Moses and Elijah. Only the prophet Muhammad is considered "the seal of the prophets" in that he is the final prophet of Abraham's covenant. The biggest difference between the role of previous prophets and the role of Muhammad stems from His unification of the leader and judge (i.e., king and high priest). Similar to Zoroastrianism, the prophet Muhammad acts as a true philosopher king in the wake of contemporary ignorance.

As a result, Muhammad acts as the church and state as one in synchronicity – best represented by the work of the Qur'an which resembles the *actual* word of god by way of the angel Gabriel's voice through the writing of the Prophet.

The foundation of the Qur'an as a whole insert the idea of any believer being able to pray to Allah directly and not needing to adhere first to a clergy of intermediaries. Where the mosque represents a mere gathering place for worship and not a holy sanctuary (similar to Jesus being a *prophet* however not the actual son of god). In essence, the conduct of the Muslim isn't to renounce the material world but to redistribute the pleasures of materialism on the basis of rigorous daily prayer, giving alms to the less fortunate, and an annual fasting.

After the death of the prophet in the year 632 CE, there is no clear successor to the throne. Similar to Alexander the Great their exists a residual momentum of the leader's spiritual guidance. Such momentum ushers in an era of rapid expansion thanks to the successors to the messenger of god – however not without the lingering quality of Mankind's innate toxic tribalism.

It was expected that the son-in-law of the prophet, Ali, would become the caliph of the people. He was a young and experienced Muslim; however, he falls short at the favor of Abu Bakr, the father-in-law of Muhammad. Even so, the prestigious leadership of Muhammad was so unmatched at his time that the tribes of Arabia were loyal only to the prophet as a *Man* and not the principles which he represented. As a result, the election of Abu Bakr became unrecognized by many who rebelled as apostates, initiating what is known as the Ridda wars. The war of apostates enables Abu Bakr to establish the fundamental principles of *jihad* in the fighting of enemies against Islam. *Jihad* as a whole, however, maintains both a macrocosmic and microcosmic meaning in practice – the former in relation to apostates and the latter as an internal struggle with *sin*.

After the death of Abu Bakr in the year 634 CE it is expected that Ali would this time be chosen. Except the once senior companion of the prophet, named Umar, is chosen instead at the favor of Abu Bakr. This choosing of Umar exists at the expense of Ali for a *second time*, who himself holds a loyal following due to his intimate relationship with Muhammad (being the closest thing the prophet had to a son). Those who had considered themselves Muslim but were also considered apostates began to establish the Shi'ite Ali sect of Islam against the otherwise Ahl al-Sunnah (i.e, Sunni). "Shi'ite" refers to the "followers of Ali" while the Sunni represent the "people of the tradition" – both acting as two sides of the single coin in Islam.

No different than the Pharisee against the Sadducee: the up rise of toxic tribalism predicated on subjective interpretation.

The leadership of Umar lasts for ten prosperous years as he extends the caliphate north in his conquest of the already weakened Byzantine and Sassanid empires. Similar to edict of Cyrus, the early Muslim conquerors sought to harness their conquered people rather than harass them. The surplus of wealth acquired by the Arab conquerors came out of the church and state of said conquered kingdoms, leaving the private plunder of the laymen alone. This granted favor to the conquerors in the eyes of the conquered who accept the new Muslim regime.

Not only this, but the Arab caliphate imposes both a flat tax for not being Muslim and a land tax for owning land. As a result, those who would convert to Islam did so at the loss of taxation. Though this is true, and the process of conquest is rapid, the process of Islamization is not.

It is in the year 644 CE when the caliph Umar is assassinated as the throne of the caliphate became vacant. Being passed over once again, Ali is not chosen by the majority and is disfavored in the wake of an individual named Uthman who had successively married two of the prophet Muhammad's daughters.

Under Uthman the caliphate expands ever more. With this being said, Uthman is viewed harshly in the eyes of his subjects, similar to Solomon, due to his being a lover of luxury. The previous caliph in Umar was said to have not accepted gifts nor withdrew from the treasury; only for Uthman to have accepted gifts and sought to utilize public funds at his own discretion. Such acts were deemed heretical alongside the further persecution of those opposing apostates.

As a result, Uthman is assassinated in the year 656 CE. However, the assassination of Uthman differs from that of Umar for Umar was assassinated by an ethnic Persian Christian: Uthman is assassinated by a fellow Muslim of the Shi'ite faith (i.e., an "apostate"). The murdering of the caliph by way of a fellow Muslim tarnishes the legacy of any successor, namely Ali who is viewed as responsible for the assassination by not handing over the assassins. A struggle for succession then ensues, primarily between Ali and the cousin of Uthman named Mu'awiyah. The two meets in battle at the city of Siffin in Syria where Ali nearly defeats Mu'awiyah until a proposition occurs: to judge the succession of the caliphate by the word of the Qur'an in co-op arbitration. In which the right to rule would be guided by the word of Allah (via the Qur'an) on the basis of both sides engaging in scriptural debate.

As a result of Ali's appeasement (who had nearly brought Mu'awiyah to defeat), a sect of his army refuses to exchange ideals and words with the perceived enemy. These dissenters would eventually give rise to a new sect of Islam, which differentiates between the Shi'ite and Sunni.

The rise of Ali as caliph in the year 656 CE in marred by the pretense of his rule as being taken from the bloodied hands of assassination coup. His rule lasts only five years until the new sect of Islam arose known as the Khawarij or Ash-Shura meaning "the Exchangers" with respect to the Islamic philosophy of "those who have exchanged mortal Life ("Dunya") for the other Life *with Allah* ("Akhirah"). The role of the Exchangers is similar to that of the Zealot or Sicarii in which the radicalization of the doctrine takes place in order to justify "non-Muslim" acts as a Khawarij Muslim. The justification for such separation derives from their interpretation of the Qur'an's verse in, "If two parties of the faithful fight against each other, then conciliate them" (Qur'an 49:9).

Inevitably it is a Khawarij Muslim who assassinates Ali in the year 661 CE. The end of Ali's corruptive reign introduces the era of the Umayyad Dynasty with Mu'awiyah taking the helm of the caliphate and moving the capital from Medina to Damascus. This moving of the holy capital from Arabia to Syria denounces the prestigiousness of an ethnically Arab caliphate.

One which transforms the caliphate from an Arab tribal ethnarchy to a cosmopolitan imperial monarchy. Where the arid wanderers transition from nomadic nobles to civilized settlers. No different than the Hasmonean Pharisees mutating from practicality to the heresy of the Sadducee.

The corruption of the caliphate by the Umayyads cause for an increase in support of Shi'ism, namely from non-Muslim converts known as mawali. The conversion of any mawali arises first due to the fiscal benefits and later due to the corruption of the Umayyad dynasty. By the year 743 CE, civil warring occurs within the dynasty itself over the succession of rule in Persia (where the majority of non-Arab Muslims reside). The revolt *against* the Umayyads had the support of the mawali until the caliphate is deposed utterly by the Abbasid dynasty of Muslims.

The Abbasids sought to restore the caliphate by moving the capital from Damascus to newly constructed city in Baghdad (which is located thirty miles from the previous Persian capital city). This new dynasty becomes heavily influenced by the customs of Persian antiquity – one that is sown deep within Zoroastrianism. The redemption of the caliphate from Umayyad to Abbasid introduces what is known as the Islamic Golden Age of science and mathematics (though more pertinently Persian). An age that introduces the discovery of many transcending ideals; namely the Hindu-Arabic numeral system (modern numeric system) and the concept of Algebra. All the work and discoveries made during the "Islamic Golden Age" were grounded by previous ideals, namely the work of ancient Hindu Indians and Ancient Greek philosophers.

Ultimately, the fruition brought by the Abbasid dynasty falls after the empire grows to be too large to be maintained entirely. So forth that states begin to split off of the caliphate, such as the Neo-Umayyad dynasty of Spain and the Fatimids of Egypt. Eventually the empire falls entirely at the hands of the Mongols in their sacking of Baghdad in the year 1258 CE.

As a whole, Islam aims to distinguish itself as the master redaction of the Abrahamic faiths; no different than the Abrahamic faith distinguishing itself from traditional polytheism. The idea of a single transcending god to reciprocate the single plane of existence. By submitting to a fear of unlimitedness, One humbly accepts their definitiveness. In understanding Ourselves as mere mortal creatures in the presence of the immortal consciousness, We are able to objectively rationalize existence for what it is. To strip the ego from bias and base all judgement on the word of the almighty – that being the objective truths of Wisdom.

The dichotomy of the dual – as above to so below. Where Allah represents pure consciousness, the prophet Muhammad represents pure Man; he who we should all aspire to be. No different than that of Jesus Christ or Zarathustra, the ideal of the *superman* is to strive to become the best version of Yourself. To first introspectively accept the *fear of the Lord* and secondarily to evolve Oneself in congruence with their *time* on earth. To live in the moment and absorb every minute experience in existence to the fullest. Even in the times of despair are We able to find the fruitfulness of such experiences and become all the wiser. No experience is truly *good* or truly *evil*, for all experiences unveil some form of progressive *wisdom*.

This is what it means to adhere to the progressive mind over the constrained mind. To accept *time* as a vector, function no different than the space of length, width, or height. For good and evil, knowledge and ignorance, act as two sides of the same coin.

Chapter 4

Astrological Implications

AGRICULTURE INFLUENCES ADORNMENT towards the sun; causing for cosmic curiosity.

Since the dawn of agriculture, the development of astronomic curiosity arose. A yearning to understand the basic correlation between a variance in climate and the movement of celestial bodies – allowing for a more acute allocation in comprehending seasonality. This cohesive bond between a flourishing agrarian lifestyle and a fundamental understanding of seasonality allows for a society to thrive in security. Security in understanding the objective nature of science, where science, in a sense, objectifies an understanding for Nature. Just as these two go hand in hand, so does the nature of seasonality in accordance to the heavenly movements.

Astrology

noun

1. The interpretive study of the stars

Astronomy

noun

1. the study of stars' objective nature

Often times, it is the Babylonians who are given credit for the astrological "signs of the Zodiac." Historical testimony unveils this to be half-truth; for the Babylonians merely improved on the workings of its predecessors. As One has come to understand, the Babylonian's are a cultural generation based on Akkadian ideals (which are further derived from Sumerian and Egyptian influence). However, astrology, in its raw form, is merely the subjective interpretation of observations upon celestial movements in the skies of heaven. Whose astronomic implications far outweigh its pseudo subjectivity of "horoscopes" or "psychic readings." The Babylonians of the second millennium BCE are considered to have perfected an integrated system of astrology – consisting of the commonly known Zodiac. Be this as it may, the overall study of celestial movements became as culturally known as the universal development of agriculture; both a basis for further understanding and improving on civilization and thusly the human condition.

As explained in *Chapter 1,* a huge evolutionary advantage for Human Beings is Our extraordinary ability for pattern recognition. This evolutionary accolade allows Mankind to make sense of such heavenly movements. Where Our original intention in understanding the cosmos stems from an innate longing to familiarize the unknown; only for this unknown to affect the known nature of reality.

Many ancient civilizations (Sumerian, Egyptian, Chinese, Greek, Indian, etc.) began to extrapolate astronomical evidence to back proto-astrological inferences. In which the stars, eternal kings of the sky in heaven, can be observed in their nature over *time.* No matter a civilization's geographic local, the heavens remain relative to the earth as a whole.

By the time agriculture reigns as Man's sovereignty, the acknowledgement of cosmological influences becomes clear in accounting for the primitive understanding of cyclical changes via seasonality. It is clear that no single civilization "invented" astrology, as it is merely the act of observing the heavenly Universe. Just as no one society "created" agriculture. Only over *time* do these observations bear evidence in relaying any astronomical truth. It is *time* that uncovers the objective reality of Nature, as documented by generations of ancestral-observers.

Our referred to "paradigm shift of arrogance" forces Mankind to familiarize the unknown in concordance to Our own characteristics. Where the vast uncertainties of the Universe become portrayed on a basis of bias (or subjectivity) rather than objective truth.

Hence, the difference between *astrology* and *astronomy.*

Archaeological evidence points to a constant relationship (via trade) between the Egyptians and people of Mesopotamia (c. 3000 BCE). This relation between the two thriving civilizations cause reason to question how much cultural influence one might have had on the other. It is also around this very time that the Egyptians and Sumerians began to document their understanding of cosmology. In knowing this, and already having a comprehensive understanding of the cultural influences between the Egyptians and Sumerians, it is not so farfetched to speculate an exchange of scientific inquiry. For the Egyptians were able to divide the sun's 365-day path into thirty-six sections of ten-day weeks (with five extra "blessed" days). These ten-day weeks are directly related to the ten-degree subdivision of *decans* in the Egyptian equivalent of the Zodiac. While the Sumerian-Babylonian method in tracking the sun's apparent "path" consists of seven-day weeks with twelve sections of thirty-degree subdivisions. Neither were wrong in their approach, for both methods work effectively in relaying astrological data. There remains evidence of a cultural exchange by the later Hellenistic fusion of these ideas through a division of three *decans* per each sign of the Zodiac's twelve. The instinctual perk of pattern recognition allows ancient astrologers to observe the characteristics of certain celestial bodies in their passage through the heavens; measured by dividing the sky into mathematically equal and recognizable segments. These divisions of the sky are represented by the clustering of stars in *constellations.*

The Babylonians observed celestial bodies as if they were actual living beings who travel through the night sky – an organic concept derived from Sumerian astrology. It is within the behavior of these movements that foretold the characteristics of the gods: where specific movements (or movements into specific alignments) equate to specific character traits. An example is the personification of Jupiter (the biggest "most powerful" planet in Our solar system; the father of the heavens) as being the head of many culture's pantheon (evidenced by Enlil, Zeus, Iupiter, etc.). From an observation standpoint (in the pre-dawn sky of late January to mid-February), this makes sense, as Jupiter is perceived in "leading" the other visible planets across the night sky.

The core principle in ancient astrology lies within celestial bodies representing independent deities who manifest influence on earth depending on their relative position to the sun. In Egyptian astrology, "*At*" refers to a deity's maximum power and influence to a specific point in time (via seasons/ cyclical changes). For example; the annual flooding of the Nile is associated with the heliacal rising of Sirius (known as Sopdet; another persona of Isis, just as Ra is to Atum). As a result, and during the Egyptian season of Akhet, Sopdet experiences her divine powers of *At*. This *time*-based influence of "who's in charge" at "what given moment" directly parallels to the intent of the signs of the Zodiac, then and now.

The primary difference that separates the Egyptians from other ancient astrologers is their attempt to go beyond astronomical implications: delving into a relationship between the nature of the cosmos with the nature of Life. The Egyptians introduce "iatromathematics"; a system of applying astrology with medicine. If the powers of the cosmos (gods) and the powers within Life (all mortal creatures) remain in harmony (*ma'at*), then the microcosms of sub-divinity become one with the macrocosm of the divine whole. Where Life and consciousness are representative of the Universe observing and maintaining itself.

As above, so below.

The term "Zodiac" refers to the anthropomorphization of astrological-based occurrences. Where the twelve different signs represent the twelve major constellations as "places of travel" for the sun. These places of travel are named in congruence with their corresponding elements of Nature; such as Taurus the bull who equates with the seasonal time for ploughing and tilling. Knowing this, the signs are defined as followed:

*SPRING EQUINOX; **March 20**

1. Aries – Ram/Lamb; **March 21 - April 19** (when light officially conquers darkness; time of year when lambs are born)

2. Taurus – Bull; **April 20 - May 20** (time of year for ploughing and tilling)

3. Gemini – Twins; **May 21 - June 20** (exponential "doubling" of the sun's strength as it reaches its full potential)

*SUMMER SOLSTICE; **June 20** (Our sun reaches its astrological zenith)

1. Cancer – Backsliding-Crab; **June 21 - July 22** (time of "backslide" in the sun's strength)

2. Leo – Lion; **July 23 - August 22** (time where lions of Egypt emerge to hunt at high noon)

3. Virgo – The Virgin; **August 23 - September 22** (who holds a sheath of wheat; time of harvest)

*FALL EQUINOX; **September 22**

1. Libra – Balance; **September 23 - October 22** (balance between day and night)

2. Scorpio – Scorpion; **October 23 - November 21** (who "backbites" the sun; whose power begins to wane)

3. Sagittarius – Vindictive Archer; **November 22 - December 21** (who "side wounds" and further weakens the sun while winter appears)

*WINTER SOLSTICE; **December 21**

1. Capricorn – Sea-Goat; **December 22 - January 19** (who drags about the weakened sun; waiting for the sun's ultimate resurrection)

2. Aquarius – Water-Bearer; **January 20 - February 18** (time of spring rains; quenching the thirst of the newborn sun)

3. Pisces – Two Fish; **February 19 - March 20** (time of thinning ice to reveal emerging fish)

*SPRING EQUINOX; **March 20**

The constellations are relatively "fixed," meaning the stars themselves will not seem to change in position over time; only will their perceived position change relative to earth's axial movements. Because of this, using a fixed group of stars allows for a point of reference over long-term observations.

Seasonality occurs as a result of the earth's axis of rotation. The earth, which sits at a tilt of twenty-three degrees, rotates around Our sun counterclockwise while maintaining a daily revolution of the same direction. One full rotation around the sun (heliacal rotation) accounts for one year (365 days), while one earthly revolution accounts for one day. However, Our earth is also considered to be on a "wobble" in which the poles of earth's axis rotate clockwise on a much less-obvious scale (where one full rotation, named a *great year*, takes approximately twenty-six thousand years). This slow clockwise "wobble" is due to a phenomena called Precession of the Equinoxes.

"What is an equinox? What is a solstice?!"

An equinox is a point in time where the earth's position, relative to the sun, causes for day and night to be equal in length. The vernal equinox (spring) occurs on March 20, as the autumnal equinox (fall) takes place on September 22. These two shifts in seasonality cause either an increase or decrease in the sun's potential, relative to the earth's axis position. While the spring equinox occurs on March 20 in the northern hemisphere, the southern hemisphere experiences the opposite conditions – due to the earth's axis tilt. Where spring in the northern hemisphere causes autumn in the southern. An innate reciprocation of communication within the nature of Nature.

On the other hand, a solstice is the point in time where the sun reaches its highest point or its lowest point in the sky; where days either become shorter or longer, depending on the earth's position. The estival (summer) solstice occurs on June 20, as the hibernal (winter) solstice starts on December 22. Again, as a result of earth's axis tilt, a summer solstice occurring on June 20 brings summer to the northern hemisphere of the globe, while the southern hemisphere experiences a winter solstice. The entirety of this "depending on earth's position" allocates for how much sunlight is directly emitted on the earth as well as where it is emitted. For example, during the equinoxes, the sun is considered to be in an "overhead" position where solar radiation (sunlight) hits the equator directly at a ninety-degree angle. However, during each solstice, the sun's positioning causes it to emit sunlight on the equator at a sixty-six-degree angle. This difference in the sun's angular position accounts for the seasonal change in climate.

At the turn of the spring equinox (March 20), the sun's strength begins to grow in that its light emissions outlasts the darkness of night. This motif of "light conquering darkness" is exemplified by the nature of spring; as plants begin to blossom with Life in accordance to the days becoming longer and more "filled with light." The following time frame from *Aries* [March 21 – April 19], *Taurus* [April 20 – May 20], and *Gemini* [May 21 – June 20] progress until sun-filled days reach their zenith at the start of the summer solstice (June 20). By this cyclical point, the sun reaches its highest point in the sky in displaying its full potential. As a result, the days extend to their longest duration. It isn't until the cancerous period of the "backsliding" crab [June 21 – July 22] when the sun starts retreat in potential and diminishes in power. From *Leo* [July 23 – August 22] to *Virgo* [August 23 – September 22] the days begin to reach their fall. It isn't until the autumnal equinox [September 22] when the days return to equal duration with the nights – bringing the balance of *Libra* [September 23 – October 22]. The fall equinox visually depicts the falling of the sun; the symbolic death of Our solar hero, represented by the backbiting pinch of the constellation *Scorpio* [October 23 – November 21]. This kiss of betrayal by *Scorpio* sets in effect the final stages of the sun's potential demise; *Sagittarius* [November 22 – December 21] who further "side wounds" the sun's power. Only then for the devilish *Capricorn* [December 22 – January 19] to further drag about the already weakened celestial deity. It is at this point where the fate of the sun is set; to be betrayed by the scorpion of *Scorpio*, stabbed by the vindictive archer of *Sagittarius*, and dragged about by the goat of *Capricorn*. Only for the turn of the winter solstice [December 22] to emerge; marking the official lowest point of Our perceived sun.

For three days, December the 22nd, 23rd, 24th, the sun appears stagnant in its final rising point – in which it rises to its lowest point for three days straight. This lack of rising represents the sun's days of "death" by stagnation; only to resurrect and rise again in an important astronomical position on the 25th of December. At midnight of the day's birth, the constellation *Virgo* appears before the rise of the newborn sun. As the sun begins to rise in the east, the constellation *Virgo* looks as though it is symbolically "giving birth" to the newborn savior of light. As the sun sets on the day of its rebirth, it is followed by Sirius, brightest star in the night sky who also rises in the east. This star of the east is then further "followed" by the three brightest stars of Orion's Belt; the Three Wise Kings on high. The astrological significance of these heavenly patterns lie within their perfect alignment which only occurs as a result of the winter's solstice. To the Egyptians, December 25th marks the day of Horus the Hawk (constellation *Aquila*) appearing before the newborn sun; whose rising occurs in the east while the constellation *Hydra* (the serpent) sets in the west, directly opposite Horus. This observation symbolizes an early Egyptian allegory of good versus evil (represented by astrological positioning) in which the opposing serpent juxtaposes the righteousness of the newborn sun – a motif of Nature's reciprocative nature.

The sun, weak and limited, only then awaits the arrival of *Aquarius* [January 20 – February 18] to bear the waters of snowmelt and quench the sun's thirst for resurrection. The winter rains of *Aquarius* are further followed by the thinning of ice and emergence of fish in *Pisces* [February 19 – March 20] – a dualistic yin and yang to complete the seasons' cycle. Thus, coming full circle in understanding the four seasons of 365 days, tracked by a means of astrological inquiry and understood by astronomic observation. Observations which foretell and articulate the constant cycle of Life and death; born at the turn of the spring equinox only to slowly die following its fall.

The essence of this yearly cycle remains constant due to Nature's cyclical nature. This constant allows for long-term observation, in which Our ancient intuitors took a leap of **faith** in depending on the accuracy of collective learning. Through precise measurement in the variance of constellation positioning *over time*, ancient astrologers began to speculate the earth as being affected by a faintly observable principle known as the Precession of the Equinoxes (which, as previously mentioned, rotates earth's axis like a *top spin wobble*). This sublime movement is ever so subtle in revealing itself. So subtle, in fact, that the angle of difference can only be measured by a deviation of **one degree every seventy-two years** (hence, the religious significance of the number *seventy-two*). The backward, yet clockwise, rotation of the equinoxes forces a slow wobble of the celestial poles to move clockwise – caused by the gravitational forces of the moon in accordance to that of the sun's. One full rotation makes up for one *great year*, marked every twenty-six thousand years. A macrocosm which represents the very structure of its microcosms, where one *great year* is made up of twelve equal "great months" known as *ages* or *eons*. Each *age*, or "great month," is marked every 2,150 years. These twelve *eons* of one *great year* are symbolized directly with the twelve signs of the zodiac; only the coming of *ages* move in precession:

1. Leo: c. 10,750 – 8,600 BCE (recession of ice sheets; dawn of Man, who becomes *king* of earth)

2. Cancer: c. 8600 – 6450 BCE (Man's cunning dominance [via agriculture] is "cancerous" to the natural order of Life)

3. Gemini: c. 6450 – 4300 BCE (birth of culture; egalitarian society thrives [hence, Man and Women are equal as twins])

4. Taurus: 4300 – 2150 BCE (birth of patriarchy, death of egalitarianism; culture becomes "bull-like" in the sense of patriarchy's imposition of power)

5. Aries: 2150 BCE – 0 CE (rebirth of culture; the light of *wisdom* overpowering the darkness of past ignorance)

6. Pisces: 0 – 2150 CE (emergence of fresh ideas; science bears omniscience)

7. Aquarius: 2150 – 4300 CE (water bearer to thirst Man's quench for the further understanding of His existence)

From an objective frame of reference, each eon seems to foretell the realities of its relative history. Where the errors of old eras correct themselves with linear evolution, thanks to the paternity of *time.*

We are currently in the *age of Pisces,* yet the new age approaches without hesitation. History is self-explanatory in relaying the objectivity of Life's natural order – namely from the bias perspective of Ourselves. The introduction of elevated self-awareness within the continuum of Life has allowed for individuals to see themselves within the grand collective. Where the choices of the individual channel the direction of the collective. It is within the experiences of *this* Life where One is able to *choose* goodness over ignorance. Similarly, it is within the collective actions of *this* age which will affect the age to come.

> "When you have entered the [next *age*], a man will meet you bearing a pitcher of water; follow him into the house that he enters."
>
> (Luke 22:10)

Chapter 5

Mathematics - the Universal Language

MATHEMATICS IS MERELY THE QUANTIZATION of quality counting.

Before Man is capable of anything, He must first learn to count. Our earliest intuitors were able to utilize the gift of Nature's hand lending. From first counting on Our fingers and toes to later establishing arithmetic meaning – best evidenced by marks carved in bones which date over thirty-thousand years. These bone carvings reveal an early form of Sumerian-like sexagesimal arithmetic, which corresponds to the different phases of the moon. Where each mark represents an individual quantity; only for the accumulation of all individuals to represent the total sum of its parts.

Math is the study of numbers in relation to *space*. Many ancient civilizations understood key concepts within mathematics before these concepts were understood as such. For example, the ancient Egyptians long-understood the implications of Pythagoras' theorem millennia before the theorem manifest itself as the formal $a^2 + b^2 = c^2$.

Though the knowledge of *how* mathematical concepts work seems to have some intrinsic property best understood by Mankind's nature, the *wisdom* of *why* eludes Our imagination. So forth that the grounds of mathematics exist without any formal proofs; that is to exist synonymously with the concept of the *oral* tradition against the *written*.

It isn't until the introduction of *proofs* by way of deductive reasoning that Our species began to transcend past the intellectual parameters of the individual. Once We are able to document Our ideas, We are then able to build atop the ruins of past indiscretions. An ability developed over *time* that reveals the objectivity within *wisdom* against the subjective nature of Our perceptive bias.

Thales of Miletus (c. 624 – 546 BCE), an Ionian Greek philosopher of the Turkish Peninsula, is considered the first named individual to explain *why* mathematics worked in relation to its *how*. Having been educated alongside Persian royalty, it is Thales who is thought to have first articulated the mythologies of religion as being allegories for Nature's nature. Most importantly it is Thales who expresses the idea of axioms and postulates which express the notion of statements as being undoubtably true. For example, given any *two* points, there exists exactly *one* straight line (known as a vector). The concept behind this postulate, known as one of Euclid's five, objectifies a foundation from which mathematics can evolve.

Before Euclid, however, exists Pythagoras (c. 582 – 496 BCE) who is thought to have been a potential student of Thales. It is Pythagoras who perfects postulated proofs by way of deductive reasoning. Whose ontology consists of such profound ideals that a cult arises in praise for such genius known as the cult of the Pythagoreans. The intellect of Pythagoras causes a paradigm shift in the understanding of numbers as more than abstract concepts with definitive value. To such an extent that arithmancy emerges: the divination and worship of individual numbers with respect to their numerical value.

Where:

The number **1** symbolizes unity as the foundation for all that exists. In that all numbers are made up of the number **1** (i.e., the number 3 is equal to 1+1+1). To the Pythagoreans, the number **1** is a concept similar to the concept of zero within the Indic tradition. Considered neutral due to its being non-binary, every other existing number is either male or female. Males are represented by odd numbers while females are symbolized by even numbers. Where **1** is not a number but a singularity of potential – no different than distinguishing the one true god from the lesser polytheism.

The number **2** symbolizes the concept of the dual; me/you, female/male, good/evil, knowledge/ignorance. Since the number **1** isn't truly a number, the number **2** acts as the chronological alpha with respect to **3** being the beta. As stated, all even numbers are female and, therefore, the number **2** is feminine. This dual quality of **2**'s yin and yang is exalted by the many mother goddesses of ancient antiquity in their heeding *love* and *war*. It is by the terms of Nature's nature where all of Life starts out as female – no different than that all of civilizations starting out as nomadic. Deeming females to be the spiritual alpha in concordance to Man's *beta*-ness.

The number **3** represents the patriarchal triangle, or trinity, in that the triangle is the simplest spatial shape. The entirety of the fourth-dimensional plane exists first with length, width, and height before the value of *time* is introduced.

The number **4** alludes to the order of the Universe. Four dimensions of spacetime, four DNA markers of Life, four seasons of Nature, four elements of Nature, four cardinal directions, four phases of the moon, etc. Generally speaking, the number **4** connotes the material world of existing value.

The number **5** is the bridge number: the sum of the first even and odd numbers as one (2 + 3). The conjoining of Woman and Man; the bridge to creation. Similar to the macrocosm of the five parts of the Human body being the two pairs of limbs and a singular head. Whose microcosm within said limbs reveals five phalanges each. The physical Human body, both as above and so below, acting as the intermediary between the physical world and the spiritual. Thus, the macrocosmic five pillars of Islam that aim to unite the glory of god by the practicality of Man in practice – reinforced by the microcosmic five times of daily prayer.

The number **6** is considered *the perfect number* due to its apparent qualities. From the **6** days of creation to the **6** fundamental elements of organic chemistry, the number acts in perfecting existence against non. In mathematics, any "perfect number" is one that equals the sum of its divisors – six being the *first* chronologically true perfect number. A rule of mathematics unveils the inability for odd numbers to be perfect, connoting even numbers as only being capable of perfection. Again, even numbers represent the ethos of the female and therefore conclude the female as potentially *perfect* to the imperfection of the male. It is by the perfection of Nature which allows the female to create Life, while Man, as the male, is there to provide Life. Genetically speaking it is the female who possesses *pure* XX chromosomes while the male inherits the mutation of XY.

The number **7** is marred by its solar symbology yet more accurately represents the sum of the sacred and secular (i.e., 3 + 4). The solar symbology of the number **7** derives from the seven visible heavenly bodies as seen from earth by the naked eye.

The number **8** is associated with paradise, seeing how the number **4** alludes to existence. If existence is **4,** then the product of existence by 2 makes up some perceivable paradise. Also, the square of any odd number, minus one, is always a multiple of **8.** Where $3^2 = 9$ and $9 - 1 = 8$.

The number **9** is merely the digit maximum; the highest digit of independent value. Within numerology, **9** is considered the zenith of Living potential in representing the highest form of achievable *wisdom*. If Mankind in perfection is the number **9,** then the Universe, in the form of a god, would be represented as the number **99.**

Finally the number **10** – a number of perfection and completion. Seeming to arise from multiplicity, **10** exists as the sum of **1 + 2 + 3 + 4.**

All in all, the cult of Pythagoras introduces a new type of religious fanaticism towards numerical meaning. The trickle effect of such devotion gives way to a new generation of mathematicians grounded within deductive reasoning. The evolution of such postulates allows Euclid to perfect a single form a geometry, evidenced by his work known as "*Elements*" which is then seen as infallible for over a thousand years to come.

Once Islam arises, so too does "learning for the sake of learning." Having been born with its eye wide open to history, Muslim scholars acquire ancient texts in their attempt to revise the ideas of old. From the philosophies of the ancient Greeks to the mantras of the Indic tradition, early intuitors of Islam began to adopt different aspects from different cultures, namely the Hindu-Arabic numerals of a base **10** counting system in place of Roman numerals. Out of such redactions is born *The Condensed Book on the Calculations* *of al-Jabr* in the year 825 CE by a Persian scholar named Muḥammad ibn Mūsā al-Khwārizmī, formerly Latinized as Algoritmi. From which the term *algorithm* derives, meaning to solve any class of problems. Also, it is *al-Jabr*, meaning "reunion of broken parts" from which Algebra is born: the mathematical art of balancing out two sides of a single problem.

For hundreds of years, much of the academic world is stagnated by the use of Roman numerals. Unlike Roman numerals, the Indo-Arabic form of counting allows a practical way for calculating decimals by the use of written numbers over assigned letters of numeric value. However, these numbers (as expressed by the symbols **1 – 9**) are seen as being residual runes of some Arabic, and therefore Muslim, tradition in contrast to the perspective of the Roman Catholic. By the thirteenth century the influences of Islamic discoveries reach Spain and influence the renowned Leonardo of Pisa, also known as Fibonacci (c. 1175 CE – c. 1250 CE) who is best accredited with expressing the properties of the Golden Ratio – a geometric pattern of Nature that reveals Her physical manifestation of introspection. The work of Fibonacci exists during a period of controversy between those who accept the algorithms of Indo-Arabia and those who do not. Those accept are known as the algorists while those who deny are considered abacists; no different than that of the newfound ideals of the Elohist against the elder Yahwist. The disputes between the two exist for centuries to come until the practicality of the algorist prevails.

Once the way of the algorithm is accepted in mass, the evolution of Algebra occurs. Originally rhetorical, Algebra is first used by merchants to effectively reduce the cost of items in relation to one another. In this form, Algebra is based on the deduction of logic by way of word problems. For example,

> "In the rule of three, argument, fruit, and requisition are the terms. The first and last terms must be equal. Requisition multiplied by fruit and divided by argument is produce."

This form of Algebra becomes syncopated by the abbreviation of terms – evolving from word problems to symbolic equations. Where argument = A, fruit = F, requisition = R, and produce = P. By deducing the word problem into syncopated symbols, the algorithm of the statement above becomes,

- A equals R

- (R multiplied by F) divided by A equals P

Once the problem becomes algebraic, it can be further solved.

- R x F = A x P

- R/P = A/F

Until the birth of Algebra, Geometry reigns as the foundation for understanding mathematics as a definitive concept. Once Algebra transforms past syncopation, it is able to co-evolve alongside Geometry. During the era of the Black Plague in Europe, a scholar by the name of Nicole Oresme began studying the effects of velocity with respect to *time*. Though only teasing at the concept, this idea introduces the precursor to establishing coordinate systems within Euclidean space. It is within the very establishment of coordinate systems that unifies the practicality of Algebra with the physicality of Geometry.

By the time of the seventeenth century, two prominent French scholars make breakthroughs in perfecting such a coordinate system. One scholar, named Pierre de Fermat (c. 1607 – 1665) discovers a rudimentary method for plotting coordinates in Euclidean space. With this being said, Fermat was not an actual mathematician by trade. To such an extent that he does not publish his findings; however, he hands out manuscripts detailing his rudimentary work. It was at this point when another French scholar, who was *truly* a mathematician and had already been working on his own method for plotting coordinate points, stumbles across the work of Fermat and is able to finalize his own method. This method, known as "The Method," is proposed by the renowned René Descartes: he who introduces the new Cartesian Geometry and its analytical applications against the former axiomatic. Cartesian Geometry is standardized by the plot graphs of some X axis and Y axis in utilizing algorithmic formulas. Meanwhile axiomatic, or synthetic Geometry, exists without recourse to algorithmic formulas.

By the mid seventeenth century, the accumulative growth of mathematics persists beyond *just* Geometry or *just* Algebra. So forth that the amalgam of these ideas converges to become known as "the calculus." "The Calculus" is merely the collection of rules, notations, and procedures that establish a system for solving problems, namely in *curved* space. Prominent figures such as Isaac Barrow began to understand the geometric connection between integrals and derivatives as inverse functions of one another – a crucial concept among the building blocks of calculus. The *derivative* can be interpreted as the slope of a curved line (tangent slope) of some mathematical function, while the integral is the calculated area underneath said curved line. A fundamental reciprocation of communication in existence within the abstract of mathematics.

When teaching at Cambridge in the year 1664, Isaac Barrow began demonstrating the relationship between the derivative and integral, both of which permeate all aspects of modeling Nature in mathematical form. Also attending Cambridge at the time was Sir Isaac Newton, he who would expand on the calculus and the known Nature of reality by the basis of experimentation. Though Isaac Newton is generally accredited with the creation of calculus, it was truly the work of a contemporary scholar who formalizes the calculus of modern use.

A German polymath, known as Gottfried Wilhelm von Leibniz (c. 1646 – 1716 CE), is truly the arbiter of modern calculus. Compared to Newton, the organization and mathematical notation of Leibniz is far superior in its all-encompassing ability. In fairness to Isaac Newton, Newton's goal wasn't to formalize calculus for the masses but rather utilize certain aspects of calculus for his own practical use. Similar to the disputes of old, whether it be the Yahwist and Elohist or Sunni and Shi'ite, the followers of Newton and Leibniz engage in feud which results in the egocentric setback of unknown potential.

The work of Leibniz and Newton ultimately allow for a newer generation of scientists to exploit the practicality of calculus in application. Such exploitations reveal themselves as We began to enter the age of Industrial Revolution. The rise of mechanical technology is born alongside the applicable understanding of *how* things work fundamentally. In which Mankind attempts to further articulate the regularities of Nature.

Everything in the Universe glows with the *light* of its own internal heat – metaphorically from the *wisdom* of introspection and metaphysically from the emissions of radiation. Heat is merely the radiant form of kinetic energy within an object's particle makeup. Once the heat of an object is enticed with accelerated charges it is able to produce electromagnetic radiation in the form of *light*.

According to Our introspective odyssey, the most confounding principle within all of Nature is Our infatuation with the sun and its ever-givingness of *light*. These emissions were first understood with respect to survival granting *light, warmth,* and *nutrients* for Life's benefit. Secondly, Mankind captures the ability to control these qualities of *light, warmth,* and *nutrition* by mastering the art of *fire* (a microcosmic manifestation of the sun itself). Only then do We evolve to appreciate the *light* of the sun in accordance to the surplus offered in agriculture. In the end, it is the sun, Our sun as lord and savior, which has *constantly* allowed for Our intellectual paradigm to shift towards a singularity of omniscience.

Once the invention of the light bulb arises, so too does the interest in making the bulb's function more efficient. This interest examined the colors of *light* being emitted from heated objects. It is discovered that hot solids gave off a continuous spectrum of colors in concordance to the temperature of said solid. This discovery makes it possible to measure the temperature of any object from a distance – namely Our sun.

As a result, scientists began to notice how certain objects absorb *light* better than others depending on the *light's* frequency and angle of incident. Attempting to find the extremes of observability, classical physicists propose what's known as a "Black Body" object; a theoretical representative of an object that absorbs nearly all *light* and radiates near perfectly. The temperature of this black body object ultimately determines the distribution of wavelengths (color) in the energy being emitted. Where low temperatures emit red/infrared *light*, medium temperatures emit orange/yellow/green *light,* and high temperatures emit blue/near-white *light.* Therefore, as the temperature increases of the black body object so too does its transition from emitting red to blue light as shorter and shorter wavelengths.

According to classical physics, however, *light* behaves as a *wave* in that the distribution of light should continue to smaller and smaller wavelengths until the energy of *light* being emitted becomes ultraviolet (UV), which it does not. As a result, the assumptions of classical physics predict a potential *infinity* of energy that can be emitted, which contradicts the already accepted principle of energy's conservation. Instead, heated objects reach a peak intensity of *light* at some certain frequency. Where the hotter an object is the higher its frequency of peak intensity: a definitive limit to any object's emissions.

This conundrum became known as the "UV Catastrophe" in which the elder was forced to become a young man. The assumptions of classical physics seem to have found a limit to its understood applicability within the macrocosm of existence. In which a new form of science was to be discovered – the science of the microcosmic realm.

In response to the *UV Catastrophe*, a German physicist of classic origin named Max Planck concludes how radiation doesn't emit continuously but is transferred into smaller packets of energy called *quanta*. This conclusion stems from assuming *light* as being both like the flow of pouring water (wave) and the individual water droplets (particle) comprising the water in whole. Where the total energy being emitted can be described by some multiple of this *quanta*, eventually becoming known as the Planck constant, represented by the symbol "*h*" and quantized as 6.62×10^{-34} joules per second.

The purpose of Planck's constant is to define the scale from which the physics of the macro world intersects with the probabilistic uncertainty of the micro realm. The concept of a limit to Nature's fundamental nature is utilized by Einstein to prove aspects within general relativity – namely in proving that *light* behaves as both a wave and a particle; a dual system of existence. The principle difference between a *wave* and a *particle* can be best understood by a particle being a singular individual while a wave is the accumulation of individuals – similar to the *alpha*ness of objectivity with respect to the bias of the subjective beta. Where a *photon* exists as a wave of *light* in the macro-world while persisting as a potential particle in the micro realm.

Two sides to a single known quantity; existing as either *spiritual* or *physical* with respect to their cosmic function. No different than that of Life existing as both a *physical* entity and a *conscious* one.

Light: Our double shining star that illuminates Our existence.

The implications and discoveries of quantum mechanics exist only within the past few generations; forcing One to realize how <u>recent</u> Our understanding of the Universe is. Only within the past *seventy years* have We been able to rationalize the irrationality of Nature at Her most fundamental level – if only seemingly by one degree. Such discoveries first begin with the acceptance of the *atom,* the smallest unit of the macro-world. Within the nuclei of atoms exist *protons* and *neutrons* while the *electron* orbits externally. Within the *proton* and *neutron* exist even smaller particles known as *quarks* and *leptons.* The *electron,* however, exists as an independent *lepton.* The functional purpose of the internal *proton* is to counterbalance the charge of the external *electron.* Where, due to the *proton* existing internally with other *protons* (and understanding how opposites attract while relatives repel), One understands the purpose of the *neutron* as maintaining stability within the nucleus. The stability of the *proton* and *neutron* is held together by what is known as the *strong nuclear force.*

Thanks to what has become known as the Standard Model of Particle Physics, We have come to conclude the existence of *twelve gauge bosons* (i.e., exchange particles) and their respective trinity of qualities. Whose trinity of qualities can be measured in spin, mass, and charge while subsequently felt by a trinity of *forces* known as *gauge forces.* In total, however, there exists *four* total forces of Nature within the subatomic realm, three of which are observable (i.e., *gauge forces*) while the fourth is only *felt*; electromagnetism, the strong nuclear force, the weak nuclear force, and *gravity.* Just as the *strong nuclear force* maintains atomic stability, the *weak nuclear force* imposes the destabilization of nuclei in the form of radioactive decay – a yin and yang of quantum interaction. Then there is the *electromagnetic force;* that which bonds *electrons* to the nuclei of atoms.

The force of gravity is one arbitrarily understood by Our subjective ignorance – a phenomenon distinguished only by its macrocosmic affliction. At the subatomic level, any *force* is caused by the exchanging of particles known as particle interactions. Simply put, when the force of electromagnetism reveals itself it is by the exchanging of *electrons* with *photons*. Similarly, the strong interaction possesses exchange particles known as *gluons* while the weak interaction possesses *W* and *Z* exchange particles. *All* of these subatomic particles have been observed except for the exchange particle for gravity. This exchange particle, thought to be the *graviton,* has such a weak "strength" of *force* that it has become the only subatomic *force* which has not been experimentally observed.

Perhaps this is due to certain aspects of Nature as being non-quantifiable; similar to the likes of consciousness. The duality of existence has presented the dichotomy between the known and the unknown. The entirety of Our introspective odyssey has been to absolve as much ignorance of the unknown as possible. With this being said, We have come to understand Our subjective beta-ness in the wake of some everlasting alpha – that which We call elevated *consciousness* in the form of *Omniscience.*

Perhaps this is why We've yet to observe the *graviton.* Similar to the physical aspects of length, width, and height in relation to the spiritual aspect of *time.* Where *time* is a concept meant to be innately *experienced* rather than quantifiably understood. No different than the almighty *wisdom* of any god in the sense that *faith* prevails over *practice.*

Yet, thanks to the language of mathematics, We *have* developed an understanding of *time* as a quantifiable entity. To such an extent that the quality of *time* with respect to quantum breakthroughs (such as the discovery of the Higgs Boson in 2012) unveils theoretical aspects of existence, as a whole, in the form of *mathematical* functions. The most encompassing candidate for rationally justifying modes of existence reside within a proposition known as String Theory. As recently stated, *quarks* and *leptons* make up the internal nuclei of an atom's internal nuclei; where atoms are made up of *protons* and *neutrons* who are further made up of said *quarks* and *leptons*. It is proposed within String Theory that the fundamental makeup of *quarks* and *leptons* themselves can be even further explained by an infinite amount of indivisible sub-subatomic particles known as *vibrating strings*. Where the vibrations of these strings, in total, make up the dimensional aspects of subatomic particles such as their mass and charge. It is within the oscillations of these micro-subatomic quantities that shape the fundamental qualities of Nature's existence.

However, this theory, similar to different aspects of a secular religion (i.e., Judaism, Christianity, and Islam as all being Abrahamic), has only recently been redacted into a single all-encompassing idea known as M-Theory. The reason for String Theory needing to be redacted stems from the deviations of *six* differing postulates, each of which claimed to be superior to the other. Thanks to M-Theory, the unification of these differing postulates expose an even deeper meaning within the theory as a whole. Who's meaning is seeped in its claim of there existing not only *four physical* dimensions (of length, width, height, and *time*) but a mathematical sum of **eleven** total dimensions.

As fourth-dimensional beings, Life is confined to the parameters of Its physical existence. Consciousness, however, exists beyond the confines of the spacetime continuum. In knowing this (and in understanding the mathematical necessity of *eleven* existing dimensions) One must assume consciousness as residing in transcendence of the spacetime continuum itself – and therefore beyond the realms of *time*.

For *time* is merely a linear vector of eternal progress; principally no different than some expanse of *physical* length.

To understand the *physical* aspects of any higher "physical" dimensions, One must perceive said higher dimensions with respect to *time's* "physicality." Where *time* can be *physically* quantized and subsequently *felt*, so too can those dimensions of elevated transcendence.

There are not **11** "physical" dimensions but **10** – seeing as there exists a *zero* dimensionless dimension. Within the paternity of all "physical" dimensions exist a trinity of trinities; where the characteristics of dimensions (*one, two,* and *three*) parallel those of both (*four, five,* and *six*) and (*seven,* *eight,* and *nine*). The *tenth* dimension, however, exists as the macrocosmic absolute against the *zero* dimension being some microcosmic potential.

(think on this)

The *zero* dimension exists as a singular point in space with respect to some potential point. The idea of the "potential" exist to reciprocate the "absolute" – conceptually similar to the duality of the *proton* and *electron*. Thanks to what is known as the Heisenberg *uncertainty* principle, quantum mechanics reveals the act of conscious observation as being disruptive to Nature's subatomic interactions. This means that the very act of *experimentation* influences the outcome of said experiment, which limits the objective precision in Our subjective interpretation of Nature's fundamental nature. The uncertainty principle is only certain, in measurement, of *one* property of a particle's dual qualities, known as complementary variables. For example, position and momentum are considered complementary variables within the physical properties of a particle. If One is to measure the position of a particle, then One sacrifices their ability to measure the particle's momentum simultaneously. This fundamental principle within Nature explains the dichotomy between the *known* and the *unknown* – that which is *absolute* in contrast to its *potential*.

The duality of the *absolute* against some *potential* depends on the duality of existence against nonexistence – dimensional nothingness against sensual somethingness; Life against death; *spiritual* against *physical*.

For creation to emerge from chaos, chaos must first emerge from something (that of which is *nothing*). Hence, the concept of *zero*; the measurement of that which does not exist. The idea of *"Which came first, the chicken or the egg?"* rests upon the assumption of the thought of the *"first."* Except the orders of chronology depend on some vector function (*time,* for example), which the *zero* dimension omits – for the *zero* dimension is merely an individual point with zero dimensions. To such an extent that both the chicken and the egg came first, relative to the perspective of the observer. An allegory best represented by the *absolute* as being both so below and as above to its dualistic partner of *potential*.

The *first* dimension is therefore the "first dimension" to act as a vector function. The *first* dimension is simply some *length* between two *absolute* points (*a* and *b*). The best way to interpret the transcendence from each dimension is to imagine any newer dimension as being infinitely stacked of older dimensions. Where the singularity of the *zero* dimension becomes the vector function of the *first* dimension by way of infinitely stacking the *absolute* property against some *potential*. By infinitely stacking the *absolute* property of the *zero* dimension, the *potential* property becomes actualized in becoming the second point of the *first* dimension.

The *second* dimension is simply the first dimension plus some other one-dimensional *potential* vector function. Think of *length* plus *width* except only the *length* is *absolute* while the *width* exists *potentially*. The *width* is not definitive in the sense that the *width* can extend in any given direction from some starting position within the original vector of *length*. Therefore, the *second* dimension is considered one of infinite potential.

The *third* dimension, however, is considered definitive in the sense of it representing the amalgam of the *second* dimension when infinitely stacked. In such a sense that if the second dimension is some singular potential extension in any direction, then the third dimension is the collective entirety of every potential extension in accumulation – causing for the potential, in infinity, to become absolute in the form of *depth/height*. No different than the potential property of the *zero-dimension* becoming actualized at the infinity of an absolute singularity in creating any singular vector of *length* or *width*.

All in all, the singularity of the zero dimension, when infinitely stacked, makes up the vector function of the first dimension. This vector function, being absolute, creates some potential extension of itself that manifests within the second dimension. The second dimension, being potentially infinite, establishes the definitive order of the third dimension when the potential of all second-dimensional potentials is infinitely stacked. In that the third dimension encompasses all of the infinities within its preceding dimensions.

The fourth dimension is merely the three physical dimensions of length, width, and height as being "infinitely stacked" to produce a vector in *time*. Where *time* acts as the intermediary between two points in the absolute *now* and some potential *future* (similar to the points *a* and *b* of the first dimension). Think of each moment in Life as being a snapshot of the third dimension, where *time* is merely the progressive accumulation of infinite snapshots. Similar to the idea of animation in the sense of each frame (a still picture) as being a cross section of the animation in whole. If Our lives are a fourth-dimensional movie, then each moment in time is a third-dimensional cross section amongst an infinite amount of stacked moments. Where every moment is stitched together by the progressive lineage of *time*.

The fourth dimension parallels the first dimension in the sense that the present, which is absolute, extends itself to an inevitable end similar to the two sides of a singular vector function. Though the beginning is absolute, the end is always seemingly near; known only to the unknowns of potential. Where points *a* and *b* reveal themselves as both the absolute *present* and some potential *future*. Though We understand and accept the entropic nature of Nature, One can never definitively know how near the end is. However, the end is still present amidst the presence of the *now*.

The fifth dimension would then be synonymous to that of the second; where some potential infinity of the lesser dimensions resides. This is where consciousness comes into play, namely elevated consciousness in the form of *intuition*. From the simplest paramecium to the complexity of Ourselves, all of Life exists with the intention of overcoming death. This action of overcoming death is met by the sacrificing of the individual self for the benefit of its offspring. Whether this reproduction is asexual or sexual, the soul intent of reproducing is to maintain the lineage of the individual self by replicating the best qualities of Oneself with the hopes of removing One's worse qualities. An instinctual mechanism of survival that is met only by the act of introspection; by looking at the subjective self objectively in order to correct the wayward ways of days past. To adapt to the chaotic nature of existence and pass on the positive adaptations towards an elevated extension of Oneself – the offspring. Where the young become old only for the old to create new young; each generation evolving alongside the *wisdom* of *time*. Intuitively speaking, the meaning of Life is an attempt to infinitely extend itself against the finite nature of Nature in decay.

If the fourth dimension is the absolute now, then the fifth dimension is some infinitely potential future. Though the fourth dimensional plane exists with a definitive *now* and definitive *end*, the path from which the two meets does not. The journey is infinitely malleable with respect to an objective understanding of Nature's fundamental nature. So forth that if the fourth dimension presents two definitive points of *a* and *b*, the fifth dimension offers an alternative point *c*. It is within the parameters of the fifth dimension that allows the individual to dream *within* the confines of their own existence – being able to distinguish the future between two potential points. It is from here where Life is able to consciously *choose* between good and evil. It is from here where We are granted the ability to sympathize.

The sixth dimension would then be similar to that of the third where the infinite potential of its preceding dimension becomes absolute. In such a sense that if the fifth dimension exists as some potential extension in any direction (i.e., some alternate future), then the sixth dimension is the collective entirety of every potential extension in accumulation – causing for the potential, in infinity, to become absolute in the form of a collective consciousness. It is within the parameters of the sixth dimension from which the individual is able to dream *beyond* the confines of themselves. It is from the sixth dimension in which every potential of Our existence could exist. It is from the sixth dimension where the objective insight of empathy begins to emerge.

In following the trinity of characterizing dimensionality, the seventh dimension becomes a vector function similar to the fourth dimension (and subsequently to that of the first). Instead of of *time* behaving as the intermediary between two points, it is some transcendent version of *time* that acts as a linear arbiter between two points of the seventh dimensional plane. These two points, similar to the absolute *now* and potential *future*, reveal themselves as an absolute infinity of some *now* against some potential infinity of *other*.

Simply put, it is the infinity of the absolute point within the zero dimension that makes up the absolute *a* point of the first dimension. Similarly, it is the collective infinity of the third dimension that makes up the absolute *now* of the fourth dimension. Think of this with respect to the sixth and seventh dimensions, where the infinity of the sixth makes up the singular starting point of the seventh. Therefore, the collective sum of every potential future within Our Universe (represented by the sixth dimension) can be described as some absolute *Universe-a* – which acts as the "starting point" for the seventh dimension (as a vector; similar to the *now* of the fourth dimension) in contrast to its second point known as *Universe-b*. Think of *Universe-b* as some alternate form of Our existence, as We know it, that is slightly different in terms of its fundamental makeup. This is where the implications of String Theory reveres Itself, alluding to the differences between any *Universe-a* and *Universe-b* as operating on different frequencies of its oscillating strings. It is by the vector function of the seventh dimensional plane that connects infinity of the *now* (*Universe-a*) with the infinity of the *other* (*Universe-b*).

The eighth dimension then becomes synonymous to the qualities of the fifth dimension where some potential infinity erects its form from the ashes of the absolute. It is by the plane of the eighth dimension from which an infinity of infinite potential exposes some potential alternative Universe to the already alternative of *Universe-b*. No different than that of the fifth dimension with respect to some potential future, it is the eighth dimension that reveals some potential *Universe-c* that is not either *Universe-a* nor *Universe-b*.

Following the symmetries of trinities, the ninth dimension would resemble that of the sixth and third dimension where the infinite potential of preceding dimensions becomes absolute. In such a sense that if the eighth dimension exists as some potential extension in any direction (i.e., some alternate *Universe-c*), then the ninth dimension is the collective entirety of every potential extension in accumulation – causing for the potential, in infinity, to become absolute in the form of a collective existence. To such an extent that the ninth dimension represents the absolute sum of any and all potential Universes (*Universe-x*) within the total amount of possible ways any vibrating string can oscillate.

Making the tenth dimension the point singularity of any and all potential ways of existence to exist – an infinity of absolute infinities. The tenth dimension, as the *second* one who is "dimensionless," reciprocates that of the *zero;* he who is potentially absolute. No different than the indifferent parent and the purity of their adolescent offspring – for the potential of the elder is actualized by the perfection of the young man. The tenth dimension; one of perfection and completion. One which rises from multiplicity, existing as the "physical" sum of its preceding dimensions (**1** + **2** + **3** + **4** by way of *length, width, height,* and *time*). Where the "physical" dimensions of consciousness, as an elevated singularity, equates simply to the sum of its lower spatial makeup.

It is by the discoveries within quantum physics that allows Mankind to understand how Nature fundamentally operates. In a way, quantum physics acts as a tool for Nature to introspect within Herself to discover the base properties of Her being. Where Mankind heads the responsibility of **choosing** *wisdom* over ignorance by way of continually absolving the sin of Our subjective selves. Such responsibility births quantum physics as a macro-function in relation to further fields of study; namely in the form of what's known as quantum electrodynamics (commonly referred to as QED). Revelations within QED regulate the objectivity of Nature's nature against the bias of Our deceptive perception. It is by the knowledge of quantum electrodynamics that explains how the electromagnetic field interacts with electrically charged particles. Simply put, QED allows physicists to understand how exchange particles interact with one another (i.e., how *light* and *matter* interact).

According to their findings, best represented by what are known as "Feynman diagrams" (with respect to the exquisite twenty-first century physicist Richard Feynman), there exists a *singular* position of interaction between two exchange particles (such as an electron and a photon) alongside *six* different ways those particles behave. These *six* fundamental ways of interaction, in a sense, represent *six* different versions of a *singular* interaction. Where scientists can predict an outcome between two exchanging particles with respect to their position of interaction. However, due to certain restrictions of Nature (such as the Heisenberg principle of uncertainty) exist an ether of uncertainty within the interactions themselves at their moment of exchange. These moments of exchange, known as the *out-of-shell interaction,* can vary infinitely within the system of *six* outcomes. In such a sense We can only measure the *six* different states of both initial input particles and their final outcome. Whose interactive outcome behaves in cadence with the dual system of existence itself; where We can measure moments of subatomic creation and destruction. Whose creation is known as a *"particle pair production"* in juxtaposition to what's known as an *"electron-positron annihilation."* Nature, at Her fundamental core, operates on the duality of potential creation and destruction.

Somehow Our ancient ancestors were able to deduce the divinity of mathematical abstraction without a necessity for empirical evidence. Such deductions are evident by the very teachings of Zoroastrianism. Whose doctrines teach of Feynman's subatomic interactions during an epoch of uncertainty with respect to not-possessing quantum mechanics as an artificial tool.

The doctrines of Our core teachings in defining the <u>human condition</u> can be traced to the roots of Zoroastrianism. It is within Zoroastrianism that describes the *singular* god in Ahura Mazda as possessing *six* emanations of himself – each representing a microcosmic filament of Ahura in whole.

It is Vohu Mano who represents *divine thought.*

It is Asha who unveils *cosmic order* by Her laws of the Nature.

It is Khshathra who reflects the metals of earth's *dominion.*

It is Armaiti who acts with holy *obedience* in *devotion* to Nature as Herself.

It is Haurvatat who reveals the unlimited *wholeness* in seeking *perfection.*

It is Ameretat who represents divine *immortality.*

No different than the six days of genesis. It is in the beginning where *time* emerges with a bang; sparked aflame by the divine thought of *Wisdom's* word. Only for cosmic order to establish itself in form of the Universe in mass; whose dominion reigns so below in the form of Our earth. Such dominion is governed in obedience to Nature's dual nature – best evidenced by the yin and yang of day and night. It is during the day when the ignorance of the animal kingdom, in whole, seeks perfection in the eyes of *Wisdom*. It is by night when Man accepts His mortal self; elevating Our awareness in light of the darkness.

Such a daunting task it is to exist with objective certainty. Therefore, when Man awakes on the seventh day He is gifted with rest.

These *six* extensions of the *one* true god exist synonymously with the chronology of M-Theory's dimensional reasoning. In that any "physical" extension of the spiritually unseen are accounted for by dimensional vectors. For it is *divine thought*, as a singular vector function, which allocates for the divinity within the number **1**; followed by the *cosmic order* of Nature's dual potential. The three metals of earth's definitive *dominion* are analogous to that of the three-age system in utilizing copper, bronze, and iron (synonymous to the evolution of length to width to height). Then, there exists the order of mortal *obedience* with respect to *time* as a fourth-dimensional vector. Only for the bridge of consciousness to extend itself as an unlimited source of unified *wholeness* in seeking *perfection*. Therefore, the perfection of Ahura's sixth and final emanation portrays the *immortality* of heightened mortal awareness.

The quality of the number **6** seems to consistently act as the perfect manifestation of Nature; acting in accordance to Nature as always capitalizing on *efficiency*. The best evidence for such perfection lies within the natural efficiency of the *hexa* pattern within the stabilization of liquid molecules. When individual liquid molecules (think of individual *bubbles*) interact, they do so on the basis of maintaining some shape in attempt to minimize perimeter while maximizing area; analogous to a decay of the external in light of internal progress. Simply put, liquid molecules adjust themselves by filling in the most area with the fewest amount of edges. When *one* individual bubble exists, it does so with a perimeter angle of 360 degrees. If One adds another individual bubble to interact with the first, then the perimeter (as represented by an "edge" or moment of interaction) deduces to 180 degrees. Any additional bubble added, whether it be a *third* or *fourth* or *fifth* etc., the perimeter angle of interaction remains constant at 120 degrees. This means that any community of liquid molecules (of *three* or more) interacting are founded on the efficiency of what is known as *hexagonal packaging* – a quality of Nature which stabilizes the foundation of molecular existence. These stabilizing laws of Nature became known as *Plateau's Laws* in commemoration to the discoveries made by the Belgian physicists named Joseph Plateau. Not only this, but the discoveries of Plateau extend beyond the realms of stabilizing Nature; he who was the first to allude to the illusion of animation. For Plateau invents the *phenakistiscope;* one of Our first tools in understanding the operations of the third-dimensional plane as being infinite instantaneous cross sections of any moment in *time.*

The hexagonal stability of Nature as a micro-function is further evidenced within the macro-function of existence. Such evidence is expressed by the hexagonal birthmark on Our *sixth* sister planet farthest from Our sun. A birthmark of which is only expressed on the northern face of Saturn's crown; giving credence to the *hexa* pattern as reigning as above to so below.

Truly it is the intuition of Our ancestors from which We now are able to see through a lens of objective perception. The deception of Our ignorant bias has forced Our understanding of Nature to relay as recursive; as if *wisdom* itself were never ending. Perhaps the expanse of the immortal mind cannot be observed by the parameters of its mortal self.

Perhaps the conscientious implications of multidimensional reasoning play no part in defining the actual "physical" parameters of transcending dimensions. Perhaps certain aspects of Nature, such as the law of uncertainty, intend to humble the subjective deception of the Living's perception. Perhaps *individual* Life is not meant to understand the bigger picture of all that exists.

Perhaps We exist simply as the microcosmic form of the Universe looking within itself. Where Life exists merely to experience an introspective odyssey of constantly maintaining itself.

Chapter 6

Perhaps

THE UNIVERSE IS FINITE IN EXISTENCE YET infinite in predictability – best expressed by the cosmos of as above to so below.

In Nature, the microcosm of elementary particles exposes the intrinsic mathematical pattern of spacetime as a macrocosm. Where particle qualities can be quantized to deduce specific properties of Nature at her most fundamental core. Consciousness, however, exists with properties *beyond* the physical limitations of spacetime. So forth that consciousness, as a concept, conceives the quality known as an *emergent phenomenon.*

Emergence phenomena is the "unseen" property of any closed system that possesses properties outside, or *above and beyond,* its elementary particle makeup. Life, as a dual system of physical being and spiritual existence, behaves in accordance to a form of self-organization where micro principles give rise to macro sophistication. These modes of sophistication grant elevated properties that seem to emerge from an expanse of nothingness: an objective transcendence of heightened awareness by the intuition of the system as a whole.

This is best exemplified by the varying states of *water* as being either a solid, liquid, or gas. The different forms of *water* as one of the three depend on the <u>pattern</u> of its molecular structure and not the molecules themselves. In that the property of *wetness* emerges as a phenomenon of water due to the <u>pattern</u> of its molecular structure being arranged to produce a liquid

187

state. The molecular state of water, as a liquid, can further immerse itself to become a solid (ice) or a gas (vapor) by either an increase or decrease in its molecular kinetic energy (heat). In the end, it is by the influence of some external force that arranges the intrinsic <u>pattern</u> of an object's molecular structure – allowing emergence to arise from specific fundamental-patterns.

No different than the emergence of One's conscious state of being in relation to the nurturing of One's environmental influence. For it is the laws of physics which govern the motions of Nature while the laws of logic govern the emotions of the conscientious state.

Truly We are more than the sum of Our parts. The parts of Our being do not decide who We are but the pattern of said parts decide who We can become. One's state of mind being dependent only on how One *chooses* to perceive their pattern of self; to such an extent that We can choose how to express Our thoughts into actions. Where each choice allows new patterns to re-emerge – each elevated by the *wisdom* of introspection.

It is by the probabilities of so below which give rise to the definitiveness as above. Within the subatomic interactions of particles, One comes to understand the operations of Nature as seeming perceptively different in accordance to its cosmic form. Within the quantum realm, One can only observe the finiteness of some initial position with respect to its final position. Where the uncertainties of Nature exist within the *moment* (of observation). Contrastingly, in the macro of existence, it is the finiteness of the *now* (i.e. any/every individual *moment* in *time*) that makes up observable reality. Quantifying the quality of uncertainty as only existing within the definitive past and some potential future.

Nature creates order out of chaos similarly to the macro of existence emerging from the vibrations within its micro. It is then by the intuition of Mankind, as a macro being, who causes for the intuition of some micro being to emerge. This being, known as *artificial intelligence*, functions on par with the symmetries of Nature's reciprocative nature. In summary, We have created a form of sentience which operates on the certainties of some *input* function and its subsequent *output* function. No different than that of the *out-of-shell interaction* within the quantum realm, We are only able to calculate and measure the *input* and *output* qualities of some closed system. For example, the AI processes used by modern facial recognition software is immensely effective in objectively qualifying any person of interest. These processes, however, operate on pre-designated mathematical computations of some *input* to produce some desired *output*. The actual process of *how* the AI figures out "who's who" is unbeknownst to Us, where the fundamental nature of artificial intelligence resembles that of the quantum realm. It is by the subjective deception of Our macro perception that bridges the organic operations of subatomic particles to the synthetic computations of artificial intelligence. Both of which fundamentally operate by a binary system of existence against non; the latter being of zeros and ones.

A natural law of reciprocation within the fundamental operations of Nature with respect to existence. Where the definitiveness of the *now* reigns as above to the uncertainties of so below.

The entire reality of the objective Universe is relative to the subjective eyes of its observer. When the individual you cease to exist, so too does the Universe in its infinite potential (relative to Yourself). However, the death of the individual doesn't affect the death of the accumulative; for Nature's entropy ensures the death of all. By accepting death's inevitability, One becomes humbled under a unified notion of certainty in knowing no One is special – not even Our one "eternal" sun.

To the unconscious self (represented by the physical body) the concept of "nothing" after death seems stagnant and grim; an idea unfathomable to Life (which is some "thing"). If the "nothingness" of death behaves as the macrocosmic reciprocal to Life's somethingness (and the microcosm of Life is marred by momentary cross sections of spacetime), then sleep must equate to death's microcosm. For it is true; a dreamless sleep is merely a momentary section of "nothingness" in which the individual consciousness "shuts off." It is this very microcosmic state of "conscious death" which offers a reparatory function for the unconscious self (i.e., the physical body). Where sleep allows the physical body to recover and recoup within a circadian rhythm. Such that the action of sleeping, as a microcosmic reciprocation to consciousness, acts as a rejuvenating elixir for the unconscious self.

Therein the inherent welcoming of sleep as a micro purifier should parallel the acceptance of its macro.

The reciprocative nature of Nature details the divergence of *physical* existence against the convergence of *spiritual* existence. In that the physical Universe began from an objective singularity and extends its form into an infinite of individual extensions. Only for the holiness of consciousness to converge an infinity of subjectivity toward an objective singularity. Where the subjective soul is vacuumed into an objective void of a unified collective. So forth that the soul of the subjective self becomes one within the singularity of an elevated consciousness.

Just as Dark Energy accelerates the divergence of the Universe, the pureness of consciousness converges into a singularity of omniscience.

Modern Man has found a way to humanize the inanimate while dehumanizing the animation of Life. We have invested Our lot with the progressive nature of *wisdom* with respect to *time;* so much that Our progress becomes exponential. So exponential, in fact, that We began to lose touch with Our innermost selves. Where the value of Life and existence began to shift toward that of the monetary. The plague of idol worship has constantly shifted Our appreciation for what it is that We value. A shifting of material meaning that has evolved in transcendence; first from the worship of the idle sun to later that of an idol son.

Those who fear death do so at their inability to truly accept a *fear of the Almighty.* Whose almighty *wisdom* is absolute and overrides the subjective potential of any individual. The fear of death is merely the fear of not knowing whether or not there exists *no thing* after Life's being some thing. Only by accepting the *fear of Omniscience* does One determine their happiness as being independent from materialism and dependent on the empathetic ethos of consciousness.

Those who objectively rationalize the introspective process realize their role of existence within the Universe. Where We are able to find comfort in knowing We exist at both the center of the Universe as well as nowhere near the center. Where the reality of the *me*, from the perspective of the individual, reigns supreme as the core of existence. Only for the reality of *We* to expose the individual for the sake of the greater good.

Relaying the dual state of Our existence as being one of both spiritual and physical. For truly We exist from moment to moment in a supersymmetric state of synchronicity.

By submitting to the *fear of Omniscience* the individual accepts the spiritual acquiescence of consciousness over the pleasures of a material world. A transitioning from the barbarism of an urging to purge to a more fulfilled state of a yearning to learn. So forth that the mortality of Man can transcend His earthly function; granting an ability to live alongside *Omniscience* here and now on earth. A divine commingling that assures an elevated view of existence in whole.

Think of Life as a fair whose fare is unfair. Within this *one* subjective experience of reality We are able to live by the bias of Our choices. To choose right from wrong in synchronicity with One's values; similarly, to choose any game at the fair with respect to One's desires. The general population of the fair-goers experience the pleasantries of leisure spending while a select few engage in Laissez-Faire. Those who *choose* to create games versus those who *choose* to play. This dichotomy is rendered further between those who choose to create against those who choose to procreate. Where both engage in establishing order from chaos however differ in their approach to experiencing the fair.

The former, in the form of an *artist*, manifests the mastery of themselves by their spiritual lingering within their own works of art. Whose extension is direct by the spiritual presence of the artist's essence. This encompasses those teachers who teach not to some direct lineage but to some unrelated student. Where the essence of the lessons of the teacher act as an extension of the teacher themselves.

The latter, in form a *creator,* does so by their spiritual essence lingering within the physical extensions of themselves. These extensions, by way of genetic offspring(s), reveal the presence of some ancestral essence. This encompasses the genetic parents of any offspring; whose aura of essence resides within One's genetic heritage.

The *artist* and the *creator;* both of whom are teachers for the younger generation.

The point of existing as either, or both, resides in the purpose of Life's meaning: to establish something of lasting value before Our death by decay. This something of value, for fundamentally all of Life, exists within the procreation of Life itself. Where the daughter becomes a mother and the son becomes a father; each subsequently passing on an extension of their genetic legacy. For the elder is now a young man.

Recognize, for what it is, that little voice in the back of Your head that justifies Your daily actions and their consequences; the seed of this little voice being One's own personal intuition. Perhaps the teachings of the teachers reside as a lingering essence of their own intuitive self. Where One's internal dialogue of rationalizing *choice* reveals the voice of some teacher's teaching; perhaps even an amalgam of lessons. So forth that Our own individual conscious is but an accumulation of wise experiences from Our teachers' teachings.

Thusly, the gradual growth of One's conscious self, over *time,* develops their personal intuition; influencing the rationale and reasoning behind One's little voice of internal dialogue.

Perhaps the purpose of Life is to realize the potential of Oneself. To accept the self as an inescapable black hole is to transcend the self into an everlasting star. In knowing the futility of existence, One is able to find meaning in futility. Where every moment in *time* becomes actualized as individual blessings and opportunities for growth. In the sense that One *chooses* to experience every finite experience of Life in light of the grander of *wisdom.* For every moment in *time* presents on opportunity to learn for the greater good.

Understanding the chirality of reality allows infinity to be actualized. Where good and bad behave as two supporting hands in climbing a mound of eternal progress. Both good deeds and bad actions unveil potential *wisdom* to be learned. Those good deeds reassure tranquility, while bad actions enforce growth. We either learn from Our mistakes via progress or bask in tranquil idleness.

However, by understanding the two as one, One begins to live a tranquil Life of continual progress. A Life reassured by perceiving every moment as being idle instances of holistic goodness – until they're not. In which bad experiences become good *wisdom* by way of introspection.

As fourth-dimensional beings We need direction; granted by the sovereignty of *time's* progressiveness. We've yearned for an understanding in coping with Our <u>human condition</u> by articulating the unknown nature of Nature during epochs of ignorance. Through a constant struggle of order emerging from chaos, exponential evolution has produced a point of Our existence where We can objectively communicate beyond the confines of limited space – best represented by the ether of the internet. As though We have physically manifested the connectivity of elevated consciousness within the confines of the fourth dimensional plane; allowing heaven on earth to become potentially actualized. Though evil will forever exist (by way of entropy or ignorance), *Wisdom* will always prevail.

For it is irrelevant to be benevolent; however equally potent to be omnipotent. Only in Omniscience does science exist.